Enemies
of your
Marriage

SECOND EDITION

MATTHEW N.O SADIKU
JANET O. SADIKU

Enemies of Your Marriage

Second Edition

Matthew N. O. Sadiku
Janet O. Sadiku

Unless otherwise states, Scripture quotations are from the New International Version (NIV) of the Bible.

Scripture quotations marked KJV are from the King James Version of the Bible.

Scripture quotations marked NKJV are from the New King James Version of the Bible.

Scripture quotations marked TLB are from The Living Bible.

Scripture quotations marked NLT are from New Living Translation Bible.

Scripture quotations marked RSV are from the Revised Standard Bible.

Cover Design by Lucas Marquez
This book is composed in Garamond

Printed in the United States of America

Matthew N. O. Sadiku and J.O. Sadiku
sadiku@ieee.org
www.matthew-sadiku.com

Published by Book Films Media
2780 South Jones Blvd Suite 200- 4007
Las Vegas, NV 89146 United States
support@bookfilmsmedia.com
+1 725-238-6534

ISBN: 979-8-9908049-1-3 (paperback)

ISBN: 979-8-9908049-2-0 (ebook)

OTHER BOOKS BY THE SAME AUTHOR

- Secrets of Successful Marriages
- How to Discover God's Will for Your Life
- Wisdom: Your Key to Success
- Choosing the Best: Living for What Really Matters
- Enemies of Your Marriage
- My Life and Work
- Radical Christian Living: By Kingdom's Principles
- Over One Hundred Loving the Word Bible Studies
- Living a Life Pleasing to God
- God is with You: Enjoy His Presence
- All Things Are Committed to Jesus
- Before Your Divorce: Read This
- Imitating God: As His Dear Children
- Matthew 1-15: A Pentecostal Commentary
- Matthew 16-28: A Pentecostal Commentary
- Mark: A Pentecostal Commentary
- Luke 1-11: A Pentecostal Commentary
- Luke 12-24: A Pentecostal Commentary

- John 1-11: A Pentecostal Commentary
- John 12-21: A Pentecostal Commentary
- Acts 1-12: A Pentecostal Commentary
- Acts 13-28: A Pentecostal Commentary
- Romans: A Pentecostal Commentary
- 1 Corinthians: A Pentecostal Commentary
- 2 Corinthians: A Pentecostal Commentary
- Ephesians: A Pentecostal Commentary
- Galatians: A Pentecostal Commentary
- Philippians and Titus: A Pentecostal Commentary
- Colossians and Philemon: A Pentecostal Commentary
- 1 & 2 Thessalonians: A Pentecostal Commentary
- 1 & 2 Timothy: A Pentecostal Commentary
- 1 & 2 Peter: A Pentecostal Commentary
- Hebrews: A Pentecostal Commentary
- James and Jude: A Pentecostal Commentary
- 1-3 John: A Pentecostal Commentary
- Revelation: A Pentecostal Commentary

IN MEMORY OF OUR LATE BROTHERS:

Olayinka David Sadiku
Olalekan Johnson Babafemi

CONTENTS

PREFACE

The divorce rate in America affects about half of all marriages. It is getting harder and harder for people to live together. This clearly shows that building a successful, long-lasting marriage is not easy.

It does not matter where you are, what you have been through, or the situation of your marriage, there is hope. God designed marriage to include you, your spouse, and Him. Without God, the Designer of marriage, you are lost in your quest for marital happiness. According to God's plan, marriage is to be enjoyed, not endured. Your marriage will thrive and succeed if you do things God's way. Do not reinvent the wheel. Learn from other people's experience by reading this book in your hand.

In our former book on marriage, *Secrets of Successful Marriages*, we share ten principles that will make your marriage work and be successful. In this book, *Enemies of Your Marriage*, we are sharing what will not make your marriage thrive. We have identified twelve enemies of your marriage. There are forces working against the success of the marriage. These enemies will truncate the life of your marriage if care is not taken. They may cause you not to enjoy the marriage and eventually lead to divorce. A marriage is successful if the couple live together happily till death separates them. The book helps you identify problem areas of any marriage and how you can overcome them. If you address these problems or avoid them, you will enjoy your marriage and be happy.

The main objective of this second edition remains the same as in the first edition: present the twelve enemies of your marriage in a manner that is clearer and more interesting. In addition, we also aim at updating the book and increasing the number of pages a little.

—M. N.O. Sadiku & J. O. Sadiku

INTRODUCTION

"Nothing feels better than a good marriage. Nothing hurts worse than a bad one." —Mike Murdock

To stay happily married is getting harder and harder these days. All marriages face problems. Couples must work together in solving the problems and saving their marriage. The authors have identified twelve common problems in marriage:

- Selfishness
- Lack of Love and Affection
- Worldliness
- Materialism
- The Devil
- Irresponsibility
- Mixed Faith
- Nagging and Criticism
- Infidelity
- Unforgiveness
- Bitterness and Resentment
- Overcommitment

Selfishness is insisting in your way or insisting on your rights. Love does not insist on its own way (1 Corinthians 13:4). Lack of love and affection is the cousin of selfishness. We cannot produce optimally where we are not loved and celebrated. Worldliness is choosing worldly priorities and spending most of our time and energy pursuing wrong goals. Materialism is a mindset that desires to make money and spend it on materials, to the neglect of spiritual matters. Satan is our chief enemy. We should be sensitive to his operation in our marriage. We should not be ignorant of his devices (2 Corinthians 2:11). Irresponsibility is not accepting responsibility for our actions.

It is difficult to cope, pray, raise kids, etc. when the couple are of different faith. Criticize sparingly and avoid nagging as much as possible. Infidelity is breaking a promise to remain faithful to a partner. Your spouse is not perfect and is going to offend you. You must be willing to forgive just as God forgives us (Ephesians 5:32). Bitterness and resentment develop as a result of pilling up offenses committed by your spouse and not forgiving them. Being overcommitted to other things and not spending enough time with your spouse defeats the purpose of marriage (avoiding loneliness).

These common problems can be avoided, fixed or resolved using many tips offered in this book. They are regarded as enemies of your marriage. These problems do not happen overnight; they creep up on your marriage gradually. If you identify them in your marriage, you should do something about them before it is late. Seek professional help if necessary.

Unfortunately most couples divorce without knowing that their marriage problems can be solved. If you address them or avoid them, you will enjoy your marriage and be happy. Your marriage will never experience divorce.

CHAPTER 1

SELFISHNESS

"Don't be selfish; don't live to make a good impression on others. Be humble, thinking of others as better than yourself"
(Philippians 2:3,4, TLB).

Before you marry, you only have one person to think about -yourself. But marriage has changed all that. Now, you have to put the needs of your spouse above your wants. For a marriage to be happy, we must avoid certain things which are enemies of happy, successful marriages. The number one enemy of your marriage is selfishness. As Oscar Wilde said, "Selfishness is not living as one wishes to live, it is asking others to live as one wishes to live."

Perhaps there is no better place where selfishness manifests itself more than at home and in a marital relationship. Selfishness is the number one enemy of marriage. It threatens oneness/unity in marriage. Marriage cannot thrive or achieve much with selfish partners. Selfishness makes it difficult to compromise. It can lead to conflict, strife, infidelity, breaking marriage vow, separation, and divorce. It causes an inability to maintain a healthy loving relationship. A selfish person goes from one divorce to another. In short, selfish people are not good material for marriage.

In our society, selfishness reigns. This should not surprise us because the Bible says that in the last days men and women will be "lovers of themselves" (2 Timothy 3:2). Although some aspects of our society may encourage selfishness, it hurts other people. There are forces in our culture that contribute and encourage selfish behaviors. These include as pornography, emphasis on individualism, personal achievement, and technology that is available for personal pleasure.

1

Marriage is not designed for selfish individuals. And God does not answer the prayer of selfish people. For example, if you pray that your spouse to die so that you claim life insurance, God will not hear you.

WHAT IS SELFISHNESS?

Selfishness is the trait that leads people to frequently act in their own interests without any regard for how their actions could affect others. It is being overly concerned for oneself or one's own advantage, pleasure, or welfare, regardless of others. It is the opposite of altruism or selflessness. They lack empathy for others. Selfish or self-centered people are overly focused on themselves.

Selfishness comes in many forms, from self-indulgence to self-pity to self-righteousness. Selfish people only care about themselves and their own needs, and they are not interested in the needs of others. They are self-centered, controlling, and manipulative. Selfishness is living by the flesh; living by sight, not by faith. For a selfish person, it is "Me, myself & I." Selfishness places you above God, spouse, and children. It is a sin against God and your spouse. God judges selfish people. A typical demonstration of selfishness is shown in Figure 1.

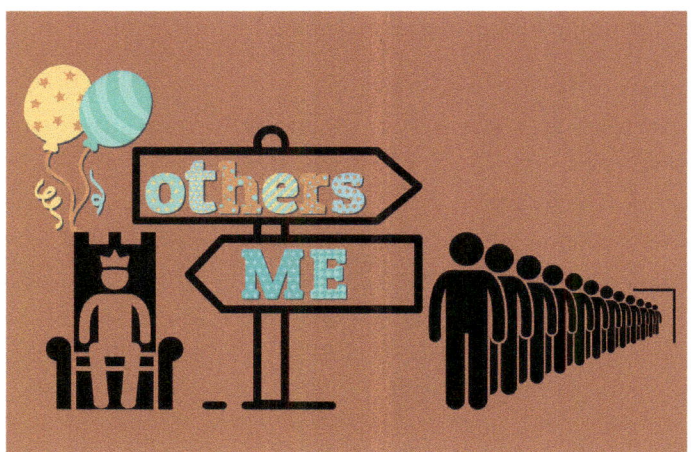

Figure 1 A typical demonstration of selfishness [4].

Source: https://pixabay.com/illustrations/selfishness-egotistical-self-love-7488645/

Samson is a good example of a selfish person. Samson was focused on himself. He prayed selfish prayers. Instead of following God's plan for his life, he went his own way. He was prideful, arrogant, and conceited. He lusted after Gentile ladies. He broke God's rules instead of serving God with humility.

By nature, we are all selfish to a certain degree. We behave in selfish or self-centered ways sometimes. But self-love and self-care are natural and part of your basic needs. They are not acts of selfishness. Experts say that most humans fall somewhere on a spectrum between pathological selfishness and extreme altruism, as shown in Figure 2.

Selfish VS. Selfless
Yandere Scale

Figure 2 Selfish–selfless spectrum.

Source: "Two critics vs. the world — Selfish vs selfless Yanderes,"

https://thatyanderecritic.tumblr.com/post/179706935142/selfish-vs-selfless-yanderes

The word of God is strongly against selfishness. Paul said, "For none of us lives for ourselves alone, and none of us dies for ourselves alone. If we live, we live for the Lord; and if we die, we die for the Lord. So, whether we live or die, we belong to the Lord" (Romans 14:7,8).

CHARACTERISTICS OF SELFISH PEOPLE

Being selfish is one of the worst character traits one may possess. Selfishness is the opposite of altruism or selflessness. It is a loser-loser game. Selfish people suffer the consequences of sins. God is not on their side. Selfishness is a sin and as such it hinders prayer since God hates selfishness. Here are some characteristics of selfish people:[1]

1. They make one-sided effort
2. They lack of empathy
3. They are manipulative

4. They are worldly

5. They are materialistic

6. They are self-centered

7. They have hidden agenda

8. They compete and compare

9. They are irresponsible

10. They make unrealistic expectations

MANIFESTATIONS OF SELFISHNESS

Selfishness is doing things in your own way or insisting on your rights. A selfish person is mainly concerned for his or her own personal welfare without caring for the welfare of others. Sometimes one can show qualities of selfishness without even realizing it. A person's behavior may be selfishly motivated without knowing it. These are the common signs of a selfish spouse:

- He cares only about his needs in bed.
- He is only interested in what pleases him; he does not help with the house chores.
- He interrupts you when speak.
- He pays no attention to details
- He cares more about career than character.
- Even when he realizes he is wrong, he does not know how to apologize and ask for forgiveness.
- She always blames others and thinks she is ok.
- She hides something she is ashamed of.
- She is sentimental, not objective.
- She keeps blaming others for her failures.

Selfishness demonstrates itself in many other ways: not praying together, having separate bank accounts, pursuing separate goals, not agreeing on the number of kids to have, one eats meat while another eats chicken, one living in Africa while the other lives in America, living as if the other does not exist, being materialistic and buying what you really do not need, cohabiting, using God's to manipulate (God told me …), having sex outside marriage, not working with your spouse as a team, etc.

Selfishness shows up in claiming entitlement or pursuing my rights. This is the feeling that I deserve something or it is my right to have a good marriage because I deserve it.

Selfishness also manifests as stubbornness, which is witch crafty. It also manifests itself in rationalization.

- What makes a teenager kill her mom? Selfishness
- What makes a husband kill his wife? Selfishness.
- What prevents a person from taking care of their parents at old age? Selfishness.
- What makes a couple not to be willing to raise children? Selfishness.

EFFECTS OF SELFISHNESS

Selfishness in any relationship can be toxic. In a marriage, selfishness gives the enemy a foothold to let in the spirit of division. Some other effects of selfishness in marriage include:

- It is perhaps the most dangerous threat to oneness in marriage.
- It repels others from you and creates an atmosphere of hatred.
- It makes it difficult to compromise.
- It leads to marital problems such as sex, communication, and in-law issues.
- It affects your happiness in marriage. It interferes with healthy selflessness which is essence of marital love.
- Prevents a couple from having the same goals.
- It can cause poor marital relationship and an inability to maintain a healthy loving relationship.
- It can prevent parents from being responsible for the kids.
- It can lead to conflict, strife, infidelity, separation and divorce.

Someone has said, "Selfishness is a fantastic way to be miserable." A good example of the effect of selfishness is shown in Figure 3.

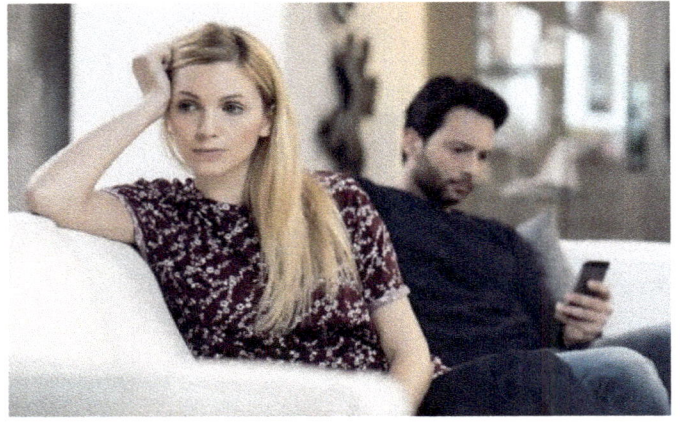

Figure 3 An example of what selfishness does to a marriage.

Source: "Top signs of a selfish husband: Why is he like that?"

https://www.lovingatyourbest.com/selfish-husband/

OVERCOMING SELFISHNESS

Selfishness is insisting on your rights, while love does not insist on its own way (1 Coritnthians.13:4). Selfishness is all about getting, while love is all about giving. We must consider others better and emulate Christ (Phil. 2:3-5). Selfishness causes disunity, disagreement, and separation in marriages.

To overcome selfishness in marriage takes time and hard work. It requires choice and determination to be selfless. I suggest that you take the following actions.

1. *Love God and His Word*

A selfish person is egocentric and makes himself a god. He considers himself as the only object of love and service. Selfish people often boast of their goodness because they fulfill certain outward moral duties. Selfishness limits a person's awareness of God. To overcome selfishness, you must choose to love God and His Word. God will heal you of the cancer called selfishness and heal your marriage as well. Submit yourself to the Holy Spirit. He will empower, guide, and correct you. He will teach you how to be selfless like Christ. You will on longer live for yourself. Your goal will be to please God in all that you do. You will desire to do all for the glory of God (1 Corinthians 10:13).

2. Self-Assessment

One important way to overcome selfishness is to assess yourself and see how selfish you are. You can be selfish in the following areas of your marriage: your finances, your use of time, your choices/ preferences, your sexual life, your relationship with the in-laws, your relationship with God, your relationship with your spouse and children, your hobbies, your career, your material possessions (house, car, cloths, etc.), to mention a few. Both of you should humbly confront the selfishness personality in your marriage. If you score low on selfishness, it means you are taking a good care of yourself and others. Keep doing what you are doing right. But if it bothers on extreme selfishness, you will need to change and do things differently. You may need to seek a professional counselor.

3. Love Your Spouse

Love is the antidote to selfishness. If you love your spouse, you will not seek your own way (1 Corinthians 13:4). If you love your spouse, you will pray for them and support them in every way. If you love your spouse, you will readily forgive them, work together as a team, and pray for each other. 1 Peter4:8 says, "Love each other deeply, because love covers over a multitude of sins." Jesus says that we should love God and our neighbor as ourself.

4. Prioritizing Your Spouse

The first step in overcoming selfishness is learning to put yourself second and prioritize your partner's needs before your own. Like Paul said, "Let each of you look not only to his own interests, but also to the interests of others" (Philippians 2:4). We must learn to prioritize our spouse over ourselves. As husbands, we are called to a higher standard that demands laying down our lives for our wives (Ephesians 5:25). Think about her needs above yours. Making her happy increases your own happiness. Make regular deposits into the memory banks of your spouse and children. They will never forget it.

Serving our husbands with a humble heart can speaks volumes. Proverbs 14:1 says, "The wise woman builds her house, but the foolish tears it down with her own hands.". God's plan is that we treasure and cultivate our marriages. Since selfishness results in being independent, sharing and giving to a spouse can be effective in breaking the chains of independence.

5. *Fight Against Pride*

Relationships flourish when we learn to relate to others in humility. As Mark Merrill rightly said, "Selfishness destroys relationships, humility develops relationships." Fight against pride by remembering everything God gives your spouse through you comes from God. Your desire to serve and your commitment to serve all come from God. Find small ways to serve your spouse-- doing the dishes, making the bed, etc. Abraham showed a humble, selfless love toward his nephew Lot by allowing Lot to choose first (Genesis 13:5-13). As Abraham exemplified, we should not seek their own good, but the good of others (1 Corinthians 10:24). As you let Jesus have His rightful place in your life, there will be less selfishness, less drama, less pride, and less me.

6. *Learn to Compromise*

Couples must understand that when they marry, it is a matter of give and take from both sides. Being selfless and loving may mean compromising. Cultivate the habit of compromising when you cannot agree on something. Let go of the need to be right or always get your way. Compromises bring you closer together.

7. *Become Selfless*

Being less selfish can bring a lot of benefits to your marriage, such as a better relationship, less stress, and more happiness. Decide to become selfless. To help you achieve that goal, recognize differences between selfish and selfless people.[2]

Selfish:

- Materialistic
- Self-promoting
- Grandiose sense of self
- Lack empathy
- Disregard for consequences
- Unkind
- Entitled
- Self-absorbed

Selfless:

- Generous
- Altruistic
- Humble
- Empathetic
- Conscientious
- Kind
- Grateful
- Charitable

Being selfless is regarding yourself as being crucified with Christ (Galatians 2:20). Paul said we should no longer live for ourselves but for Christ (2 Corinthians 5:15).

CONCLUSION

Act more like a teammate and less like an adversary. Commit to playing cooperatively versus competitively. Become a team player in your marriage. Unity is the goal of Christian marriage. God wants husband and wife to be united in purpose to glorify Him while maintaining their uniqueness. That goal cannot be achieved with selfishness but with love; love is selfless, not selfish. If you pursue this goal, you will enjoy your marriage and be happy.

We end this chapter with a quote from Dalai Lama:[3]

"If you think only of yourself, if you forget the rights and well-being of others, or, worse still, if you exploit others, ultimately you will lose. You will have no friends who will show concern for your well-being. Moreover, if a tragedy befalls you, instead of feeling concerned, others might even secretly rejoice. By contrast, if an individual is compassionate and altruistic, and has the interests of others in mind, then irrespective of whether that person knows a lot of people, wherever that person moves, he or she will immediately make friends. And when that person faces a tragedy, there will be plenty of people who will come to help."

NOTES

1   Marissa, "7 signs of selfish people (and how to deal with them)," May 2022,

https://atozenlife.com/selfish-people/

2   K. Cherry, "How to stop being selfish," January 2023,

https://www.verywellmind.com/how-to-stop-being-selfish-7096599

3   J. White, "7 Strategies I'm using to become less selfish & more selfless," April 2020,

https://www.mindbodygreen.com/articles/how-to-be-less-selfish

CHAPTER 2

LACK OF LOVE AND AFFECTION

"Don't just pretend that you love others: really love them. Hate what is wrong. Stand on the side of the good. Love each other with brotherly affection and take delight in honoring each other"
(Romans 12:9,10).

More and more Americans live alone than ever before.

Love and affection are essential to our daily health, just like food and water. However, we do not get as much love and affection as we need. Just as lack of food, water, and rest have their detrimental effects, so too does the lack of love and affection. Love and affection are considered essential components in any relationship.

Healthy relationships are important to individuals and the society as a whole. Lack of love and affection in marriage can be a grave misfortune to any man or woman because it deprives them of the greatest joys life has to offer. This deprivation is an enemy of marriage and it may surely destroy the relationship.

Although no relationship is perfect, affection is an important part of any loving relationship. It is the verbal and physical expression of the love, warmth, happiness, and caring you and your partner feel for each other. It allows us to connect to another person by showing our feelings.[1]

WHAT IS AFFECTION?

By nature, humans require love and affection from others, whether in close relationships or with a larger group of people. Love and affection can be essential for human development and reducing loneliness and isolation in every stage of life. The importance of affection and love can vary depending on an individual's lifestyle, experiences, and preferences. However, going without love and affection can have physical, mental, and emotional consequences.

Loneliness and social isolation in adults have been shown to cause chronic health conditions. As illustrated in Figure 1, everyone needs love and affection, regardless of your age and gender. Every person deserves to be loved and appreciated.

Figure 1 Everyone needs love and affection.

Source: "The importance of affection and love in relationships,"

https://www.betterhelp.com/advice/love/the-importance-of-love-and-affection-in-your-life-and-relationships/

Love is a deep and strong affection whereas affection is a feeling of liking and fondness. Affection is any action intended to arouse feelings of love in the giver and recipient. Affectionate behavior could be kissing, holding hands, hugging, or having sex. Love may be regarded as a strong and deep affection. Love is always associated with positive feelings like caring, warmth, and happiness. The main difference between love and affection is that love is deeper and stronger than affection.

Feelings of love and affection carry with them numerous health benefits by lowering your blood pressure, stabilizing your mood, encouraging bonding, reducing pain, and creating an overall calming sensation. To love and to feel loved can feel as significant as other basic needs such as food and drink. Love is a living thing that you can kill or cherish and it bears fruit. A loveless marriage results when you kill love. A happy marriage results when you cherish love. Love is the target Satan attacks in marriage. God's Word will help you develop love.

AFFECTION DEFICIT

Here are some of the signs indicating lack of affection or affection deficit:[2]

1. There is no spark of playfulness between you
2. There are little or no displays of mutual gratitude
3. Communication mostly centers on the mundane
4. There is little or no touch between you
5. You talk negatively about your partner to others
6. You feel you don't love your partner any more

Women tend to love men for their character, while men love woman for their appearance. Just as our body craves for food, water, and rest, so does it crave for affection. Figure 2 shows a couple where affection is lacking.

Figure 2 A family without love and affection.

Source: "Signs of lack of affection in children,"

https://steemit.com/steemiteducation/@jorgelis23/signs-of-lack-of-affection-in-children

Affection can be one of the first things to go when a marriage is in trouble. If you are craving affection in your marriage and are longing to be hugged, kissed, or given affection through caring words such as "I love you," you are not alone.

All relationships require affection to survive. When affection is gone in a relationship, you will feel a loss of the old bond you shared. As affection declines, the chances of relationship to survive in the long run also declines.

ROOT CAUSES

The root causes of the pain must be addressed before your relationship can move forward to a healthier, happier, more intimate place.

Any marriage can be saved from a lack of affection provided the couple want to improve or change. At the foundation of overcoming lack of love and affection is the couple's desire to preserve the marriage and family.

The first step toward recovery is to confront harmful ways of thinking and behaving, and replace them with healthier methods. Seek appropriate counselors or pastors, resources such as books, videos, and couples' workshops.

Begging for affection feels terrible, even if your man or woman comply! So my advice is: do not do it. Fretting about a lack of affection won't help you save a marriage or make your marriage more affectionate. So focus on what you can control.

INCREASING YOUR LOVE AND AFFECTION

When someone is part of your life for the long haul, such as a spouse, parent, child, or friend, it is all too easy to take the relationship for granted. Here are some ways to enhance your love and affection and not take your partner for granted. These are tips that make relationships survive and thrive.

1.   *Communication:* You should be able to talk to your partner about anything—the good and the bad. This is important for a healthy relationship. In your communication, be honest, truthful, and open with your partner. It is important to be able to talk together without

fearing how they will respond or if you will be judged. For example, if you want your partner to be more loving and affectionate with their words, feel free to let them know. Affectionate communication has many benefits such as intimacy, satisfaction, commitment, and long-term survival.

2.   *Commitment:* Love is a voluntary, intelligent choice, made in the full knowledge that the opposite choice (selfishness) is always possible. It is a commitment of the will. Commitment is the glue of marriage. It is having the intention to persist in a relationship. It is what makes a relationship strong. It is what your marriage vows are all about. It may involve taking responsibility for your actions and words. It may also involve spending time together or just talking together.[3] The amount of affection you express to your partner best predicts your commitment. Sometimes, you need to verbally communicate your commitment to your partner. Remember, you are the one who gains when you are highly committed to your marriage.

3.   *Respect:* You need to mutually respect each other. Without respect, your partner might not prioritize the relationship and may refrain from listening to you. Instead of giving and receiving love, feelings can be hurt, and resentment may build over time. If respect is present in your relationship, your partner will value your beliefs, opinions, and who you are as a person. You should treat each other as equal partners. You have the same say in making decisions. This will make you and your partner feel important and respected.

4.   *Physical affection:* To avoid your relationship becoming a routine, you need to be more romantic or affectionate. Physical affection is an important aspect of romantic relationships. Different ways you can show affection include hugging, massaging, caressing, cuddling, holding hands, kissing on the lips, kissing on the face, and touching. Other ways include a greeting card or an "I love you" note; a bouquet of flowers; phone calls; and conversations with thoughtful and loving expressions. Recent research has shown that increased kissing in relationships is linked to decreases in cholesterol. Physical touch is also a key factor to a lasting relationship. Showing physical affection enhances closeness and commitment. This increases relationship satisfaction which in turn leads to greater sexual satisfaction. There is less conflict in romantic relationships when partners treat each other with physical affection. An example of a couple showing physical

affection is shown in Figure 3.

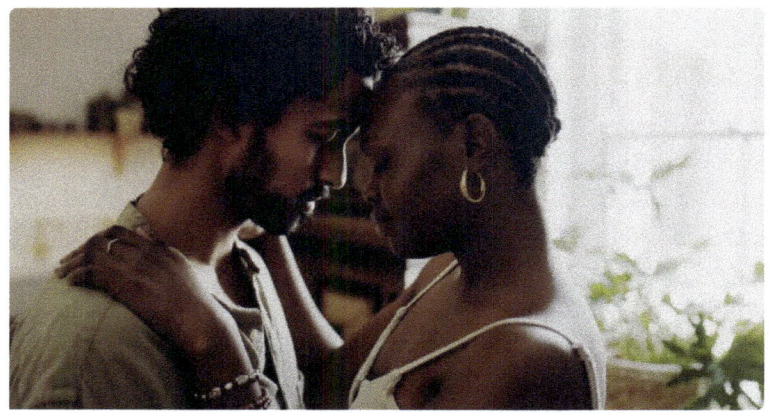

Figure 3 A couple showing physical affection.

Source: B. Field, "How to show affection in a relationship," August 2022,

https://www.verywellmind.com/how-to-show-affection-in-a-relationship-6272274

5.   *Be there:* You may see each other infrequently as you are busy with other things in your life. You can only create time for affection in a relationship when you are available. Your basic daily events should not deprive you of taking time to be with your partner. Going to work every day, attending to businesses, traveling, or attending to the children and house chores can take a toll on your time. Showing love and affection sometimes just means being there is enough. You will be surprised by how supported your partner feels when you take time out of your schedule to be with them for occasions big and small.

6.   *Show Affection:* Affection means a lot in a marriage. It is the expression of caring for your spouse. When you show affection toward your spouse, it sends the message that they are important to you. Without it, you leave your spouse feeling disconnected and alone. There are so many ways you can demonstrate affection to your partner. These include the following:[4]

- Hugging
- Kissing
- Cuddling
- Holding hands
- Patting someone's back

- Wrapping your arm around another's shoulder or waist
- Sending cards and gifts
- Reassuring someone when they are down
- Discussing the positives in the relationship
- Offering to be there if someone is depressed
- Cracking a joke if you and a loved one are in a disagreement

CONCLUSION

Affection and love are important mediators for our mental health and wellbeing. A romantic relationship can lose its love and affection at any time if care is not taken. This can negatively affect our happiness, ability to work, and physical wellness.

Hopefully with the tips given above, you can stir your marriage in the right direction and feel like your relationship is growing in a positive way. Great marriages do not happen by coincidence. They are the result of a consistent investment of time, affection, forgiveness, and commitment between a husband and a wife. Love is a decision, not a feeling or infatuation. Understand your spouse's basic needs and be willing to meeting them. Show love in words and deeds. When your wife is truly loved as Christ expects you, when she knows that she means more to you than anything or anyone else, she is fully under your control. Someone has said, "A woman will leave you for lack of attention and affection quicker than she would if you cheated on her."

If you struggle with showing affection or have a spouse that does, you can benefit from counseling. You can seek the help of a marriage counselor or medical professional. Seeking help can save your marriage. The books[4, 5, 6] can also be of help.

NOTES

1   M. T. Hill, "Intimacy, passion, commitment, physical affection and relationship stage as related to romantic relationship satisfaction," *Doctoral Dissertation*, Oklahoma State University, May 2009.

2   Rich Nicastro, "Strengthen Your Relationship,"

http://www.strengthenyourrelationship.com/free-relationship-resources/free-relationship-advice-articles/relationship-advice-does-your-relationship-suffer-from-affection-deficit-disorder/

3   M. N. O. Sadiku and J. O. Sadiku, *Secrets of Successful Marriages*. Bloomington, IN: iUniverse, 2nd edition, 2022, p. 162.

4   B. Field, "How to show affection in a relationship," August 2022,

https://www.verywellmind.com/how-to-show-affection-in-a-relationship-6272274

5   L. D. Grace, *Love and Electronic Affection: A Design Primer*. Boca Raton, FL: CRC Press, 2020.

6   S. Gerhardt, *Why Love Matters: How Affection Shapes a Baby's Brain*. Routledge, 2014.

CHAPTER 3

WORLDLINESS

"Do not love the world or anything in the world. If anyone loves the world, love for the Father is not in them. For everything in the world—the lust of the flesh, the lust of the eyes, and the pride of life—comes not from the Father but from the world"
(1 John 2:15,16).

There is a great danger of worldliness in the midst of our churches. Today, worldliness is one of the biggest principal challenges facing the church worldwide. There is too much worldliness among Christians. In the world today, it is becoming increasingly difficult to distinguish between Christians and unbelievers. Instead of being radically different, too many Christians are copying the ways of the world and in the process, they become worldly. Gospel music is becoming increasingly secularized. Ladies are painting themselves and distorting the image of their bodies. The message of holiness and repentance is no longer common. It is time to say no to worldliness among Christians.[1]

The Christian marriage stands in great danger from the forces of worldliness and materialism. Worldliness is a terrible problem for mankind and for marriage particularly. Worldliness is a dangerous enemy of yours and your marriage. Any Christian who lives in America is susceptible to this terrible plague of worldliness. Christians are not opposed to making money or making their way in this world. We are not indifferent to improving oneself through education or training. What we are opposed is choosing the wrong priorities in life and spending most of our time and energy achieving the wrong goals. Let us begin this chapter by clarifying what worldliness is all about.

WHAT IS WORLDLINESS?

There are two ways of viewing reality: through the prism of the world, and through the prism of the Spirit. We are either worldly or godly. The way of the world is hostile to the things of God and 180 degrees removed from the love of righteousness. Worldliness is the love of beauty without a corresponding love of righteousness. According to Jesus, the world's way seems to be appealing, broader, and easier (Matthew 7:13).

Worldliness is not a matter of dos and don'ts. Rather it is a matter of the attitude of the heart, the attitude of life in thinking and dealing with things. Worldliness manifests itself in our lives in the following ways.

1. *Worldly Mind-set:*

Worldliness is a man-centered way of thinking. It is to be secular, unspiritual, materialistic, and irreligious. It is the mind-set of the unregenerate. It is nothing more than self-centeredness. It urges us to get what we want, when we want it, and how we want it. It is focused on self, not on God or others. For example, if a lady wears a new dress in church in order to attract attention, that is worldliness. If a man must buy a new car every year in order to keep up with the style, that is worldliness. Worldliness operates from the flesh, which lusts against the Spirit (Galatians 5:17) and the carnal mind which is hostile to God. It judges the importance of things by material results. It measures success by numbers.[2] This is fundamentally the basic difference between the person of faith and the unbeliever. The unbeliever judges things by worldly standards, by his senses, and by time. The believer brings God into everything, viewing things from His perspective.

To avoid cultivating the worldly mindset of their neighbors, God specifically told Israel not to act like other nations (Jeremiah 10:2). They paid no attention to this in many ways. They asked for a king to lead them like other nations (1 Samuel 8:5). They were involved in evil practices exceeding the pagan nations they displaced (2 Chronicles 33:10). God was so angry with them that He sent them to exile (1 Chronicles 9:1).

2. Worldly Wisdom:

The wisdom that comes from the world is earthly, unspiritual, and demonic (James 3:15). It's tempting to follow the advice of worldly wisdom because many times it seems to make sense—at least from man's point of view. Worldly wisdom thrives in the culture of lies and deception. The world promises to make people happy with pleasures, materialism, and instant gratification. Yet the world's wisdom only leads down the road of disappointment, regret, and pain.

3. Friendship with the World:

The whole world's system is anti-God. It generates and sustains our government, entertainment, fashion, business, healthcare, education, technology, and legal system. It profoundly affects our belief systems, values, and attitudes, and these in turn have shaped our conduct.[3] Worldliness is being more concerned about worldly affairs than spiritual things. It is the exact opposite of godliness. Paul equates worldliness with spiritual immaturity in 1 Corinthians 3:1-3. Demas deserted Paul because of worldliness (2 Timothy 4:10).

Friendship with the world is hatred toward God (James 4:4). We cannot love both God and the world. We must make a choice. Paul said, "Do not copy the behavior and customs of this world, but be a new and different person with a fresh newness in all you do and think" (Romans 12:2, TLB). We should be in the world and yet not of the world. We should not fear what the people of the world fear or become like them (Isaiah 8:12, NIV). The tragedy is that when we become like the world, we lose all our power to influence the world.

4. Satan's Influence:

Satan is the god of this world (2 Corinthians 4:4). Worldliness is Satan's use of idols such as pride, selfishness, and pleasure to maintain his dominion over men and women. It is one of the greatest challenges facing churches today. Worldliness thrives in the environment of lies and deception, which are the tools of Satan. Instead of the churches transforming the culture, the reverse has happened. Unconsciously, churches have been converted to the world through worldliness. The church is asleep spiritually and not paying attention. Satan has designed ways of life that are fast-paced, filled with an array of sense-appealing entertainments, fashions, and gadgets. Because of its subtle attractiveness and magnetism, worldliness has impressed itself upon

God's people and had a stronghold on most marriages. Much of the spiritual deadness and complacency in our churches and marriages finds its roots in worldliness.

Other ways worldliness manifests itself include worldly manners (2 Corinthians 1:17), worldly passions (Titus 2:11,12), worldly cares (Matthew . 6:25-33), and worldly love (1 John 2:15).[4] Figure 1 typically shows what worldliness is all about.

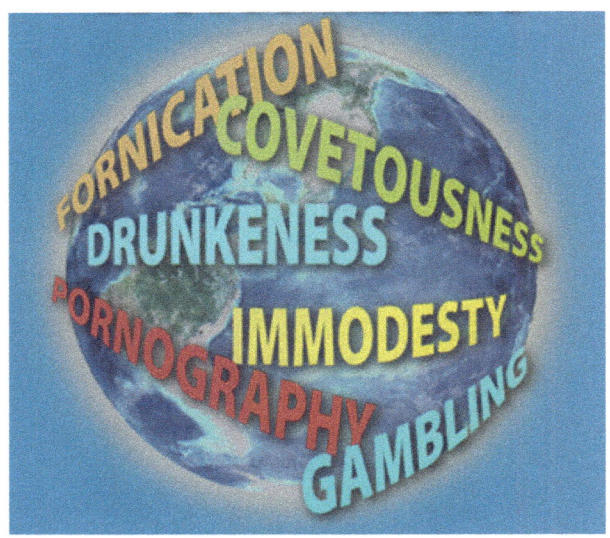

Figure 1 The essence of worldliness.

Source: P. Robertson, "Abstain from worldliness (teen/adult 3:3),"

https://onestone.com/products/abstain-from-worldliness

CONSEQUENCES OF WORLDLINESS

Worldliness has some negative effects on your marriage and your soul. These include loving the world, accumulating materials unnecessarily, and hostility to marriage.

1.   *Loving the world:* Worldliness withdraws our affections from the nobler things and fix them on earthly things. Christians are warned not to love the world (1 John 2:15). They should live in the world, but not be filled with it. But if the world gets into them, they lose their influence. If worldliness should come in, godliness would go out. As Kevin DeYoung rightly said, "Worldliness is whatever makes sin look normal and righteousness look strange."

The world is cosmos, a system apart from God, being organized and regulated upon ungodly principles and false values. Loving the world is having a lingering desire to be part of the world after one has been saved from it by Christ. It is becoming seduced again by the very things that once held us captive.

According to 1John2:15-17, worldliness is the lust of the flesh (sensualism), worldliness is the lust of the eyes (materialism), and worldliness is the pride of life (egotism).[5] Worldliness makes us to be ungodly engaged with the world. It focuses our attention on earthly "accomplishments" and materials- cars, homes, clothes, gold, diamonds, money, beautiful women, etc. It distracts our attention from preparing for Christ's return and makes us focus on worldly things. Figure 2 illustrates a worldly activity.

Figure 2 A typical worldly activity.

Source: W. Jackson, "What is worldliness,"

https://christiancourier.com/articles/what-is-worldliness

We should remember Lot's wife. She looked back, revealing that her heart was still to be in Sodom, a type of the world. She reluctantly left Sodom because she loved the world, not having the faith in what the angel told her (Genesis 19:26). She gradually believed that the angel's expectations were too exacting and difficult and she suddenly died.

2.   *Materialism:* Worldliness gives birth to materialism. We live is a dreadfully materialistic world. Materialism has compelled mankind to pursue unsatiable desire and unbounded greed to achieve more and more which results in a disgraceful life of immorality, immodesty,

pornography, drugs, child abuse, women abuse, divorce, and other kinds of social misbehavior. Man has become obsessed with striving for more comfort, more material goods, greater power over his fellow men, and unceasing technological progress. Advertising (a tool of 'phenomenon of consumerism') has been accused of promoting and glamorizing values that are materialistic and self-centered. Advertisers have focused more on people who yearn to be free from all restraints and responsibilities.[6] Materialistic people spend all or most of their time working and striving for material things. They care not for the true and eternal riches of God. Christmas is a good example of the world's power of attraction through advertising. It plays upon all of a person's senses with pleasant music, lights, colors, foods, clothes, gifts, and parties. It is an attractive trap to worldliness.

This passionate, unrestrained pursuit of material goods, to the exclusion of everything else, bars man from all spiritual insight and close walk with God. It leads to lack of satisfaction, frustration, unhappiness, lack of fulfillment, and confusion.

3.   *Enemy of marriage:* Worldliness has a power that produces an intriguing result in marriages. The world thinks of marriage as "game over," and marriage has become materialistic. Marriage is regarded as a means to an end and an end in itself in the everlasting struggle for status and stuff. People think sexual pleasure is the most important thing in the world. Sex is awesome and wonderful, but we should not make it a god.

4.   *Division:* Worldliness also causes division in the church and in a marriage. Some Christians have legalistic tendencies: they see almost everything as worldly. Since love of the world is probably the number one reason for apostasy in the church, we need to find balance between world flight and worldliness. What is worldly activity for the wife might not be worldly activity for the husband. May God give us wisdom.

OVERCOMING WORLDLINESS

Identifying what worldliness is one thing, battling it is quite another. To escape worldliness, we must apply God's way of escape. We must imitate Christ, develop a strong faith, focus on things above, share things with others, and be watchful.

1.   *Imitate Christ:* We are called to be like Christ. We are to

increasingly resemble the character and nature of Christ. Jesus Christ is not a conformist. We are called to be the light and salt of this world (Matthew 5:13-16). A light that conforms to the darkness renders itself useless. Salt which loses its saltiness is good for nothing. We should be exemplary in their character and conduct. Husband and wife should imitate Christ and serve each other as unto the Lord. They should follow the steps of Christ (1 Peter 2:21). In any situation, they ask themselves: "What would Jesus do?" They should provide a good example for their children.

2.   *Develop a Strong Faith:* Faith is the victory over the world because through our faith we let go of the world and cleave totally to Jesus. "For whatever is born of God overcomes the world. And this is the victory that has overcome the world--our faith." (1 John 5:4) Faith comes as God's world is implanted into our hearts (James 1:21). "Do not love the world or the things in the world. If anyone loves the world the love of the Father is not in him (1 John 2:15).

3.   *Focus on the Things Above:* To escape worldliness Christians are taught to: (1) to avoid a love of the world (1 John 2:15-17), (2) keep yourself pure and clean (1 Timothy 5:22), (3) put to death sinful habits (Colossians 3:5-6), (4) to say "no" to ungodliness and worldly passions (Titus 2:11-12), (5) seek the things that are above (Colossians 3:1).[7] God demands that we have more allegiance to Him than to the members of our own families (Matthew 10:37-39). We must not let the world around us squeeze us into its own mold (Romans 12:2). If we love God, worldly things would not have much appeal. We should no longer seek the things that are of the earth – the lust of the flesh, lust of the eyes, and pride of life. We are now to align ourselves fully with our citizenship in heaven. We must live as though our home were in heaven (I Peter 2:11). Our longing to commune with Christ and be with Him should control all that we do.

4.   *Share With Others:* God is not against His people prospering or even getting rich. For example, Abraham, David, and Solomon were wealthy beyond imagination. We are only trustees or stewards of all God has given us and we are expected to be faithful in distributing the wealth (1 Corinthians 4:2). God wants us to share what we have with others – the poor, needy, widows, orphans, foreigners, etc. God is most concerned about how we use our wealth to further His kingdom and how we work within our relationships with our spouses

and others.

5.   *Be Watchful:* We must constantly realize that we are in enemy territory (John 17:15, 1 Peter 5:8). To avoid being useless in our life and ineffective in our marriage, we need to be watch and prayer. The enemy uses worldliness to undermine our faith and corrupt the truth. There are several things in this world that fight for our time and can make us lose our focus. Supernatural influence has to be met with supernatural power: 'For though we walk in the flesh, we do not war according to the flesh. For the weapons of our warfare are not carnal but mighty in God for pulling down strongholds' (2 Corinthians 10:3-4).

CONCLUSION

Worldliness is one of the most dangerous enemies of a believer. It is one of the greatest enemies of marriage. Worldliness is basically a matter of motives, attitudes, and values. As Christians, we must be radically different. We should not allow the pressure of our society have any negative influence on our beliefs or practices. We need to examine ourselves and see how worldly we are. You want to make your marriage to become better? Become more godly and do it God's way, not world's way. 1 John 2:15 says, "Do not love the world or anything in the world. If anyone loves the world, the love of the Father is not in him." Choose to live free from worldliness and temporal pursuits. Instead bear fruit that will last for eternity.

For the Christian marriage, the choice is clear. Husbands and wives must avoid worldliness in all its forms at all costs. Our goal is to allow the Holy Spirit to take charge our life and become insensitive to the lusts of the world. Our lifestyle must confirm to that of Jesus, who we are supposed to be imitating. More information about worldliness can be found in the books.[8-10]

NOTES

1   Vicky, "Worldliness among Christians,"

https://www.vickysforum.com/worldliness-among-christians/

2   I. H. Murray, "Worldliness," July 2000,

https://banneroftruth.org/us/resources/articles/2000/worldliness/

3   John W. Ritenbaugh, "The world, the church, and Laodiceanism,"

https://www.cgg.org/index.cfm/fuseaction/Library.sr/CT/CGGBOOKLETS/k/452/World-Church-Laodiceanism.htm

4   C. McDowell, "8 important Bible verses about worldliness,"

https://www.whatchristianswanttoknow.com/8-important-bible-verses-about-worldliness/

5   V. C. Grounds, "Loving the world: Rightly or wrongly," Christianity Today, vol. 24, no. 007, April 1980, p. 20.

6   M. Prewitt, "The true worldliness of advertising," Theology Today, vol. 60, 2003, pp. 384-396.

7   C. Box, "At a time of extraordinary materialism is urgency to avoid hell of worldliness,"

http://www.spirit-digest.com/Life-after-life/TheOtherSide/worldliness.htm

8   C. J. Mahaney (ed.), Worldliness: Resisting the Seduction of a Fallen World. Crossway, 2008.

9   W. F. Pinar, The Worldliness of a Cosmopolitan Education: Passionate Lives in Public Service. Routledge, 2009.

10   R. J. Mouw, Called to Holy Worldliness (Laity Exchange Books). Fortress Press, 1980.

CHAPTER 4

MATERIALISM

"Do not store up for yourselves treasures on earth, where moths and vermin destroy, and where thieves break in and steal. But store up for yourselves treasures in heaven, where moths and vermin do not destroy, and where thieves do not break in and steal"
(Matthew 6:19,20).

As mentioned briefly in the previous chapter, materialism is one the greatest enemy of marriages, especially in America. America is a country that guarantees life, liberty, and the pursuit of happiness for its citizen. It prides itself on individualism and its concept of the American dream. Opportunities are everywhere. A person can start from nowhere, work hard, follow the rules, and be successful. The idea that material possessions improve one's personal and social well-being permeates America.

Unfortunately, the American dream is becoming more and more materialistic. Today, there is an endless lists of things that people want: the latest smart phones, luxury cars, designer shoes and bags, Rolex, etc.[1] Wives or husbands who put a lot of weight on luxury vacations or designer décor may end up not being the perfect match in marriage.

There is even an underlying assumption that there is a direct correlation between wealth and success, wealth and power, wealth and spirituality. Even Christians begin to think that if God loves them He will bless them with a temporal blessing. We cannot help but have a materialistic mindset in America. And materialism is ruining us. As illustrated in Figure 1, does money or material possession control us?

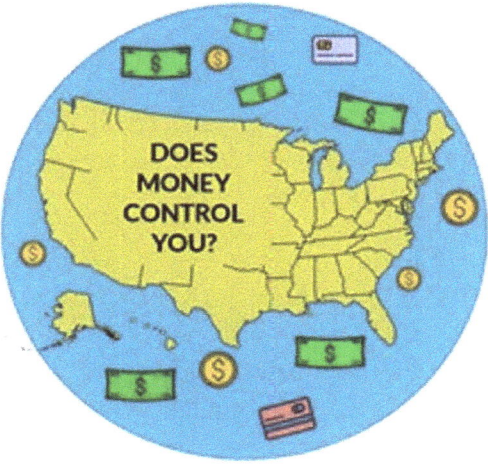

Figure 1 We will always want what we cannot have.

Source: "Let's stop glorifying materialism,"

https://macshieldonline.com/25179/opinion/lets-stop-glorifying-materialism/

Through technology, globalization has brought nations together as a village and introduced significant changes in peoples' lifestyles and values. Materialism has become a global phenomenon through modernization and westernization. The developing countries being envious of the western world are feeling the pressure of making money and reflecting materialistic tendencies as the developed economies.

WHAT IS MATERIALISM?

Materialism is part of the American way of life. It defines us, motivates us, and moves our economy more than any other custom. We are constantly taught by society that the more we have, the more we are worth, the better we look, the happier we will be. Keeping up with the Jones' is a standard way to describe the goal of the average American. As with all things, materialism has its good and bad points. Some of our basic needs are best met by materials. There is no substitute for a good umbrella on a rainy day. A smart phone provides convenient communication. But some people place a disproportionate high value on things to meet their needs.[2]

Materialism refers to a preoccupation with material objects, comforts, and considerations with no interest in spiritual values. It may be regarded as a worldview or philosophical system which regards matter as the only reality in the world. Since materialism denies the existence of God, it relies on Darwin's theory of evolution to explain itself and is incompatible with most world religions, including Christianity, Judaism, and Islam. No religion is against material success gained the right way. Religion only opposes the wrong way we can use it.

Materialism is a mindset that desires to make money and spend it on materials, to the neglect of spiritual matters. It is a lifestyle with a high degree of material consumption. It is the act of attaching high value and importance on consumer goods and worldly possessions. It is giving higher priority to obtaining, maintaining and protecting material objects than we do in developing and enjoying interpersonal relationships. It represents the way people value things such as money, clothes, and social status more than things like knowledge, discovery, and education. It is foolishly chasing the wind (Ecclesiastes 2:26). It can make or break a marriage. Materialism tends to strain marriages. Married couples who save together, spend together, and stay together.

Materialism manifests itself in many ways: obsessive accumulation of unnecessary products, elementary school children having iPhones, teen suicide, depression, disintegration of the family, divorce, bankruptcy, and despair. Job said that the evil man may accumulate money like dust, with closets jammed full of clothing (Job 27:16, TLB). A materialistic person is not the ideal person to have a relationship with. A materialistic woman is every man's nightmare; so is a materialistic man. Figure 2 shows an example of materialistic couple.

Figure 2 An example of materialistic couple.

Source: "7 Signs of a materialistic woman,"

https://www.elcrema.com/7-signs-of-a-materialistic-woman/

Materialism is commonly connected to the notion of culture since it varies substantially across cultures. Countries having a collectivistic culture (such as India) show less prone attitude towards materialistic things than to those following individualistic culture (such as US).

WHAT CAUSES MATERIALISM?

Many Christians would deny that they are materialists. Yet they live as if material things and physical comforts are of utmost value. They talk of heaven but strive for earthly things. We will consider four major causes of materialism in marriage: our personality, neighborhood (peer pressure), media, and technology. These are the key sources of materialistic values.

1. *Personality:* Personality refers to the basic regulatory mechanisms underlying individual behaviors, attitudes, beliefs and values. As far as materialism is concerned, there are two kinds of goals people may have: (1) extrinsic goals which focus on external rewards and are motivated by consumer culture and opinions of others, (2) intrinsic goals which tend to satisfy inherent psychological needs that all people have. Extrinsic goals tend to diminish the quality of our lives, whereas intrinsic goals promote greater health and more social justice.[3]

2. *Influences of Neighborhood:* We are often tempted to copy those around us. We try to "keep up with the Joneses." For example, if we see our neighbor driving luxury cars, we are likely to feel a need to spend money we may not have to project an image of wealth we do not actually possess.

3. *Influences of Media:* Although wealth plays a major role in being materialistic, the media influences decisions in our everyday lives. Advertising constantly bombards us with the newest gadgets. We must avoid the traps of advertisements because "they want your money." Even children as young as two show preference for advertised brands. In America, holidays (such as Thanksgiving and Christmas) have come to be about shopping and buying new things. To businesses, holidays are about making money and luring consumers to buy their products by lowering their prices

4. *Influences of Technology:* We live in a marketing-driven and increasingly digital media society. The increase in high tech, digital devices in the areas of household appliances (laptops, microwave oven, TV, etc.) has changed the landscape of the American home and family. Digital commerce now allows one to buy and sell goods and services using the Internet and mobile devices. Facebook, Instagram, Twitter, and similar social media are effective instruments of peer influence. These media strongly suggest what you must own to fit in and be considered acceptable. American households will continue to pursue these material goods to satisfy their need for comfort and entertainment.

IMPLICATIONS OF MATERIALISM

Materialists regard possessions and acquisition as essential to their satisfaction and well-being in life. They judge themselves and others by the amount of possessions accumulated. The consequences of materialistic tendencies include debt, sadness, and fake happiness. Materialistic values cause a lot of other problems such compulsive and impulsive spending, increased debt, decreased savings, financial turmoil, depression, social anxiety, less satisfaction, vulnerability, insecurity, non-generosity, and unfulfillment. They can make you lose your perspective, your money, and your morals. They can also lead to unnecessary jealousy and competitiveness, which can cause stress. That is too great a price to pay.

We will consider four of these major problems that have negative effects on your marriage.

1.   *Relationships suffer:* Every kind of relationship falls into this category: spouses, friends, parents, siblings, school mates, children, co-workers, etc. All the values that we cherish in relationship - such as love, truth, compassion, and justice - evaporate in a culture of superficiality, which materialism breeds. Money becomes the ultimate arbiter between people. The worth of a man is seen only in terms of how much he brings regardless of the means employed. The love of money becomes the root of evil (1 Timothy 6:10). Not only do our personal relationships suffer, our spiritual relationship suffers as well. God blesses us, we become prosperous, and then we abandon Him. We often make wealth our god, not the true King of heaven.

2.   *Marriage strained:* Materialism causes disaster for a marriage. It likely has harmful effects on a couple regardless of whether the value is shared by both husband and wife. Materialism is harmful in marriage for two main reasons. First, materialism may cause spouses to spend money unwisely, thus creating financial stress in the marriage. Second, materialistic spouses place a high priority on money and are less focused on their marriage relationship.[4]

Materialism is causing human connections as in marriage and friendship to be lost and for the human experience to become less meaningful. It is also linked to less effective communication among married couples, higher levels of negative conflict, lower relationship satisfaction, and less marriage stability.

Studies have shown that the more we love things, the less we want to marry and have kids. There is also an agreement today that money is a key factor in a large percentage of marital conflicts. But the real culprit here is materialism – an underlying assumption that money can buy happiness and success for couples. The quest for more things and the lack of enough money is a stressor that destroys homes and families, even Christian homes.

3.   *Debt increases:* Materialism can lead to accumulating debt and financial turmoil. It has been associated with credit card misuse. New credit cards come in every day, everyone wanting to lend us money, wanting to help us refinance our homes, pressurizing us to buy more and more. The availability of credit card has eliminated the need to

postpone acquisitions and defer gratification until a time when people can pay with the money they have saved. The proliferation of credit cards and their ease of acquisition ensure that even college students today have opportunities for making credit purchases. Using credit card can lead to compulsive buying behavior, in which a consumer feels an uncontrollable, a chronic urge to shop and overspend to show their status and affluence. As Will Rogers well said: "Too many people spend money they haven't earned, to buy things they don't want, to impress people they don't like."

Perhaps the best way to end this sections is going over

"15 Things Poor People Do That The Rich Don't:"[5]

1. Poor people watch a lot of TV.
2. Poor people eat fast food.
3. Poor people buy clothes or products that on sale.
4. Poor people wake up later than rich people in their early years.
5. Poor people are really into sports.
6. Poor people don't shower as often as rich people.
7. Poor people blame others for their misfortunes.
8. Poor people have no money saved.
9. Poor people use credit cards or take out a loan for useless things.
10. Poor people tend to have kids earlier in life than rich people.
11. Poor people do not do regular checks with their doctor.
12. Poor people spend money before they get it.
13. Poor people surround themselves with other poor people.
14. Poor people never follow through their ideas or potential.
15. Poor people believe that others should help them reach the top.

4. *Unhappiness:* A materialistic person is vested in owning material possessions and thinks material possession brings happiness. In reality, materialism brings us unhappiness and anxiety, indicating that material possessions are not the solution for a happy life. The risk of financial resources is often demonstrated by the suicides and emotional breakdowns that commonly occur during significant drops

in the stock market. Materialism is the mother of perpetual insecurity. Happiness comes as a result of making godly choices.

OVERCOMING MATERIALISM

If you are materialistic and you want to cut down, there is hope for you. Here are five suggestions to combat materialism.

1.   *Minimalist Lifestyle:* Some people begin to hate others just because they have nice things which they do not have. Negative feelings arise from materialism and cause sadness and jealousy. Simplify your life and live a minimalist lifestyle. The minimalistic lifestyle is all about living with less, as an alternatives to materialism. You need to understand the difference between your needs and wants. Minimalism encourages people to let go of things that they can do without. It has many benefits such as getting out of debt, having less stress, and being environmentally friendly. Adopting a minimalistic lifestyle is not easy; it takes a lot of time, convincing, and determination.[6]

2.   *Expressing Gratitude:* The first step in combating materialism is that you must be grateful for the circumstances that brought your wealth and focus on the community that surrounds you. We have many things that some people in other countries can only dream about. We must avoid greed and be satisfied with what we have. Christians who are determined to follow Christ should understand where their treasure really is. We must take time to think of things heavenward. We must be careful not to set our heart on things that really do not matter. For example, if certain sports begin to adversely affect your family commitment, then pull the plug immediately. As Ali Talib rightly said, "Detachment is not that you should own nothing. But that nothing should own you."

3.   *Setting Priority:* Marital relationship usually fairs better when spouses share priorities and values. Husbands and wives should sit down and make a number of choices that help in this regard. Jesus said, "Is not life more important than food, and the body more important than clothes?" (Matthew 6:25b). We should transcend the spirit of materialism and remain vigilant against the danger of losing what is more valuable. Spend more meaningful time with your partner.

Minimize the exposure of your children to media at early age. Children easily get fascinated towards unrealistic belongings promoted by ads and persuade their parents to purchase them. Unfulfilled requests of children for materialistic things make them unhappy, which may result in conflicting situation in the family. The results of materialism on children is illustrated in Figure 3.

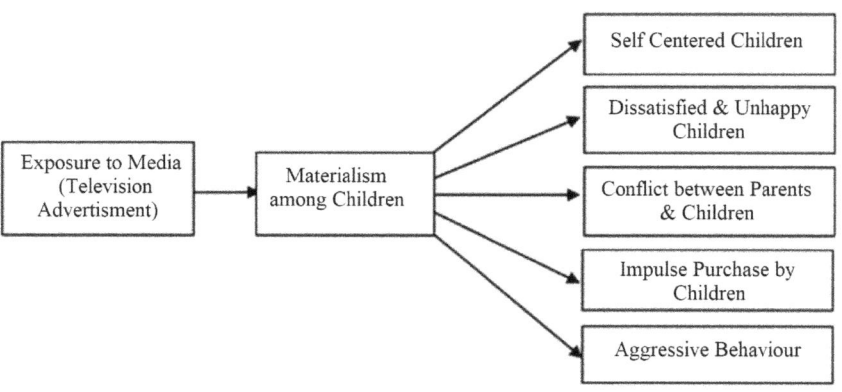

Figure 3 Effects of materialism on children.

Source: Vandana and U. Lenka, "A review on the role of media in increasing materialism among children," *Procedia - Social and Behavioral Sciences*, vol. 133, 2014 , pp. 456 – 464.

4.   *Be Contented:* Godliness and contentment make us wealthier than material possession. "Yet true godliness with contentment is itself great wealth. After all, we brought nothing with us when we came into the world, and we can't take anything with us when we leave it. So if we have enough food and clothing, let us be content. But people who long to be rich fall into temptation and are trapped by many foolish and harmful desires that plunge them into ruin and destruction. For the love of money is the root of all kinds of evil. And some people, craving money, have wandered from the true faith and pierced themselves with many sorrows" (1 Timothy 6:6–10). Seek first the kingdom of God and He will give you the desire of your heart (Matthew 6:33).

5.   *Sharing with Others:* Generosity is the biblical antidote to materialism. Inequality in America is becoming increasingly prevalent and the gap between the rich and the poor widens. As depicted in Figure 4, materialism goes hand in hand with poverty in America.

Figure 4 Materialism and poverty in America.

Source: M. Greenwood, "Materialism and Ppoverty in America," April 2021,

https://sites.manchester.ac.uk/global-social-challenges/2021/04/29/materialism-and-poverty-in-america/#:~:text=Materialism%20is%20a%20major%20factor,their%20material%20belongings%20with%20others.

God created us to love people and use things, but materialists love things and use people. We are only a trustee of what God has given us. Whatever we possess will not remain with us forever, because we will pass away from this world empty-handed. "After all, we didn't bring any money with us when we came into the world, and we can't carry away a single penny when we die" (1 Timothy 6:7, TLB). As you give and share your resources with others, you are storing up treasures in heaven (Matthew 6:19,20). "If anyone has material possessions and sees a brother or sister in need but has no pity on them, how can the love of God be in that person?" (1 John 3:17).

We must learn about materialism from the rich fool in Luke 12:13- 21 and replace selfishness with selflessness. We must learn to share and donate items that we do not really need to those who are less fortunate – the poor, needy, widows, orphans, foreigners, etc. As Billy Graham well said, "God has given us two hands, one to receive with and the other to give with."

CONCLUSION

We all have material things, but it can become a problem when we become obsessed with them or let them control us. Materialism is the tendency to consider material possessions and comfort more important than spiritual values. It is the importance that people attach to worldly possessions. Today, Americans thrive on materialism and we never seem to have enough. They lead the world in the culture of material consumption. Materialism has made Americans selfish, ungrateful, greedy people. Although materialism itself may not cause marital failure, commercial debt it can create is "an equal opportunity marriage destroyer." So do all you can to prevent materialism from killing your marriage and keeping you out of heaven. More information about materialism can be found in the books.[7-14]

NOTES

1   S. Khurram, "Is the American dream becoming too materialistic?"

https://naturevscivilization.weebly.com/is-the-american-dream-becoming-too-materialistic-by-shanzeh-khurram.html

2   M.L. Richins, "Materialism pathways: the processes that create and perpetuate materialism," Journal of Consumer Psychology, vol. 27, no. 4, 2017, pp. 480–499.

3   Lisa Mastny, "Consumerism, values, and what really matters: an Interview with Tim Kasser,"

https://newdream.org/blog/2011-07-kasser-consumerism-values-and-what-really-matters

4   D. Gibson, "How materialism harms a marriage," October 2011,

http://www.foryourmarriage.org/how-materialism-harms-a-marriage/

5   "15 things poor people do that the rich don't,"

https://www.youtube.com/watch?v=swjSycfB4Gw

6   A. Ragavanis, "Materialism and minimalism: The benefits of a new lifestyle," June 2019,

https://lhshorizon.com/3576/opinions/materialism-and-minimalism-the-benefits-of-a-new-lifestyle/

7   G. Scott, The Materialistic World: How to Escape Materialism, Theory of Materialism, Mindful Living, Living with True Happiness. CreateSpace Independent Publishing Platform, 2015.

8   G. E. Romero, J. Pérez-Jara, and L. Camprubí (eds.), Contemporary Materialism: Its Ontology and Epistemology. Springer, 2022.

9   K. N. Cameron, Dialectical Materialism and Modern Science. Intl Pub, 1994.

10   S. Bergmann, K. Rigby, P.M. Scott (eds.), Religion, Materialism and Ecology. Routledge, 2023.

11   M. Ghadirian, Materialism: Moral and Social Consequences. George Ronald Publisher, 2nd edition, 2017.

12   P. Virno, Convention and Materialism: Uniqueness without Aura. The MIT Press, 2021.

13   W. Blanton, A Materialism for the Masses: Saint Paul and the Philosophy of Undying Life. Columbia University Press, 2014.

14   J. Reader, Theology and New Materialism: Spaces of Faithful Dissent. Springer, 2017.

CHAPTER 5

THE DEVIL

"We do not wrestle against flesh and blood, but against the rulers, against the authorities, against the cosmic powers over this present darkness, against the spiritual forces of evil in the heavenly places" (Ephesians 6:12).

A lot of things could be working against your marriage: your spouse's mistakes, your own inadequacies, differing personalities, different expectations, conflict of interest, busyness, sickness, extended family problems, just to name a few. But none of these are the real enemy of your marriage. Some couples erroneously believe that their spouse was their enemy. Recognizing the real enemy is Satan, not your spouse, is a vital step to take in spiritual warfare. Ephesians 6:12 says, "For we do not wrestle against flesh and blood, but against principalities, against powers, against the rulers of the darkness of this age, against spiritual hosts of wickedness in the heavenly places" (NKJV).

Your marriage is under attack whether you realize it or not. Every marriage is going through spiritual warfare. The enemy is real. Your spouse in not your enemy; he or she is your ally. Satan is the enemy of your soul. Satan is working through humans to destroy the fabric of society, the institution of marriage. We are engaged in a spiritual war against an invisible enemy. For though we walk in the flesh, we are not waging war according to the flesh. For the weapons of our warfare are not of the flesh but have divine power to destroy strongholds. (2 Corinthians 10:3-4). Figure 1 shows an example of how a believer is in spiritual warfare.

Figure 1 A believer is in spiritual warfare.

Source: "Spiritual warfare,"

https://www.cslewisinstitute.org/resources-tag/spiritual-warfare/

The Bible says that Satan prowls around like a lion looking for someone to devour (1 Peter 5:8). Sometimes Satan sneaks into your home to do havoc. He comes to kill, steal, and destroy (John 10:10). His ultimate aim is to destroy your unity as a couple, diminish your love for your spouse, and ultimately make your marriage fail so that God's purpose for your marriage is not achieved. If Satan fails to destroy a marriage, he will try to weaken it and make it less effective. By this we mean that Satan will prevent the marriage from achieving its intended purpose. He understands that strong families raise up a strong next generation.

In this chapter, we will briefly discuss who Satan is, how he operates and what we can do to defeat him.

WHO IS SATAN?

Some Christians believe that the history of Satan is described in the Bible in Isaiah 14:12-15 and Ezekiel 28:12-19. The devil goes by many names: Satan, Lucifer, the Prince of Darkness, ruler of the demons, the god of this world, and adversary of God. The word "Satan" is the English transliteration of a Hebrew word for "adversary." Thus, Satan simply means adversary. The image in Figure 2 is used to depict Satan.

Figure 2 Satan, our archenemy.

Source: https://stock.adobe.com/search?k=satan

Satan was the greatest of all the angels created by God, but he rebelled against his Creator. Pride originated from his desire to be God instead of a servant of God. Satan pitted his will against God's will and led a revolution among the angels. According to Revelation 12, one third of the angels followed him. He was cast from heaven and became a fallen angel. God has sealed his ultimate doom (Matthew 25:41).

The fall of Satan shows that angels and human beings can become evil if they so choose. Throughout history, some have disavowed the existence of Satan as a real, personal, spiritual being. Satan himself likes that. But belief in a literal devil and demonic possession remains strong among Pentecostal Christians.

Satan is a wicked being. He strongly opposes every institution of God such as marriage. Ordinarily, we are no match for him. We must let God fight our battles for us and give us victory (Deuteronomy 20:4). If we let Him, He will be an enemy to our enemies (Exodus 23:22, Message).

HOW SATAN OPERATES

Satan hates what God loves. He hates you. He hates Christians. He hates marriages. He hates Christian marriages. Satan desires to destroy your marriage. His agenda is clearly stated in John 10:10: "The thief comes only to steal and kill and destroy." We should not be ignorant of his devices (2 Corinthians 2:11). How does Satan destroy marriages? Satan's methods of operation include deception, temptation, instilling doubt and fear, and materialism.

1.   *Deception:* As a deceiver, Satan disguises himself in many forms: as a serpent, a doubter, a lion, etc. Deception is the greatest weapon the prince of darkness relies on. This is the tool Satan used to deceive Eve in the Garden of Eden and fractured the first marriage (Genesis 3). He is crafty and shrewd in his operations. He delights in deception. He seeks to lure individuals and couples into his traps. The devil may deceive you that you are married to the wrong person. When he brings accusation against your spouse, remember that Satan is the "accuser of the brethren" (Revelation 12:10), When your marriage seems not to be doing well, it is tempting to begin to focus on the faults of your spouse. The enemy is good at identifying our weak spots. He is upset at the commitment you made at your wedding, and he is doing everything in his power to make you feel like you made a mistake. He uses emotions and anger to lead us into sin. Through deception and perversion, Satan uses inordinate sexual relations to gratify carnal desires. His grand agenda is to control mankind. He deceives people by saying that "What you don't know cannot kill you." He convinces people that he does not exist. Do not believe his pack of lies. Figure 3 shows how the devil deceives.

Figure 3 How the devil defeats.

Source: B. Cereno, "things people get wrong about the devil,"

https://www.grunge.com/268331/things-people-get-wrong-about-the-devil/

2.   *Temptation:* It is a comfort to know that Satan cannot tempt us through a multitude of channels but can enter our lives through only three gates (1 John 2:16):[1]

- the lust of the flesh,
- the lust of the eyes, or
- the pride of life.

When Satan comes to tempt an individual, he must appeal to one of these basic characteristics of human nature—its carnal capacity, its selfish interests, or pride. Jesus was tempted in these three areas, yet did not sin (Matthew 4:1-11, Hebrew 4:5). Satan could not reach Job through any of these gates because Job was blameless (Job 2:3).

Because we are prone to put ourselves in situations where we subject ourselves to Satan's attack, we are advised to:

Put on the Lord Jesus Christ, and make no provisions for the flesh, to gratify its desires (Romans 13:14).

We ought to safeguard our minds and hearts so that we do not provide that which Satan can use to produce sin in us.

Above all else, guard your affections. For they influence everything else in your life (Proverbs 4:23, TLB).

3.   *Doubt and Fear:* Like a roaring lion, Satan uses fear to intimidate a believer. He uses fear to instill doubt and unbelief in a believer's mind. He does that in many ways. He makes us anxious about our needs and makes us doubt whether God will provide for those needs and if He even cares about us at all. The fear of not having our needs met is destructive because it threatens our very existence and our marriage. Satan also uses the fear of death to intimidate a believer. He makes us fear the loss of our own life or the life of a loved one. When Satan intimidates us with the fear of death, instead of nursing the idea, we should rebuke him and start praying for the loved one. We must tell him our rights in Christ:

No weapon forged against you will prevail (Isaiah 54:17).

Whoever touches you touches the apple of his [God's] eye (Zechariah 2:8)

Your life is now hidden with Christ in God (Colossians 3:3).

Since our life is "hidden with Christ in God," Satan cannot touch our life without first touching God. The apostle John wrote, "You, dear children, are from God and have overcome them, because the one who is in you is greater than the one who is in the world" (1 John 4:4).

4.   *Materialism:* The devil can induce a husband or wife to put too much emphasis on pursuing career, houses, cars, and material wealth. Our society is saturated by materialism, hedonism, and egocentrism, having the material things and false sense of security. We already covered materialism in Chapter 4.

OVERCOMING THE DEVIL

Satan hates marriage and seeks to destroy it. To counter Satan's attack on marriage, we must understand God's design for marriage and how to oppose Satan's schemes. We overcome the enemy using the Word of God, prayer, sexual intimacy, putting on God's armor, and seeking help when needed.

1.   *God's Word:* Our greatest defense is the Word of God. When tempted by the devil, our Lord Jesus Christ defeated the enemy by quoting Scriptures (Matthew 4:4,7,10) Husband and wife should be filled with God's Word. They need the wisdom from God's Word to defeat the devil. The Word of God is the power that overcomes the devil. It is a powerful, spiritual weapon we need to fight the enemy. We need to operate with faith in the Word of God, His promises.

2.   *Prayer:* Satan desires that we cease communicating with God and one another. Prayer is our lifeline. Marriage is from God, about God, and we neglect God at our peril. When you pray, you walk in your God-given authority and you have power over your enemy. When things are not going well in your marriage, talk to God about them and ask for His intervention. He will supply the strength and wisdom we need to successfully do battle in our marriages. As you pray for your spouse, confess your failures. Of course, we do not need to wait till we are in trouble before we pray for our marriages. In spite of what you are going through, you must constantly lean on God. The first and best thing you can do restore or strengthen your marriage is to PRAY.[2]

Pray for your home.

Pray for your mate.

Pray with faith.

Pray with boldness.

Pray with persistence.

Pray with authority.

Pray against the devil.

3.   *Sexual Intimacy:* Husband and wife owe each other sexual intercourse on a regular basis. Paul commanded: "Do not deprive one another…. So that Satan may not tempt you because of your lack of self-control " (1 Corinthians 7:5). Forgive your spouse if he or she has done something wrong. This will keep Satan from getting advantage over you. To safeguard against Satan's temptations, couples must engage in regular, joyful sex. You will not hate your spouse when you pray and have sex together on regular basis.

4.   *Putting on the Armor:* We must constantly be aware of the fact that our warfare is not physical but spiritual and that it takes spiritual weapons to fight it. We must understand our enemy's tactics and use the right weapons to defeat him. That is why we need the armor of God. Paul commanded us to "be strong in the Lord and in the strength of his might" (Ephesians 6: 10). This is achieved when husbands and wives "put on the whole armor of God" (v. 11). We are in a wrestling with Satan and his demons (v.12). But the battle really belongs to the Lord and we must engage Him. The victory is determined beforehand and the last hour is settled.

In Ephesians 6: 10-12, Paul focuses on six indispensable pieces of the armor: belt, breastplate, shoes, shield, helmet, and sword. They respectively stand for truth, righteousness, readiness of the gospel of peace, faith, salvation, and the Word of God. Each piece of the armor pertains to a specific spiritual truth on our identity in Christ. The sword of the Spirit, the Word, is unique because it is the only offensive weapon in the arsenal. We need to arm ourselves with the Word.

5.   *Resisting the Devil:* Although Satan can coerce, deceive, and tempt, he cannot override man's free will (James 1:14,15). Each time the devil tempted Him, the Lord's resistance was couched in the repetitive refrain: "It is written…" (Matthew 4:4,7,10). The Bible tells us that we can resist the devil and he will flee from us (James 4:7).

6.   *Seeking Help:* If you have tried everything and a marital problem cannot be resolved, you need to seek help. You are not alone in your fight; you are part of the larger community of faith. Involve your pastor, brethren, and close friends. It is not a sign of weakness to seek counsel. It is easier and less painful to learn from the experience of others. Our plans fail or succeed depending on how informed we are in making them (Proverbs 15:22). Other people who are not directly involved in an issue can look at it more objectively than we can. As the wise man said, "Where there is no guidance, a people falls; but in an abundance of counselors there is safety" (Proverbs 11:14).

CONCLUSION

Christian marriages are involved in spiritual warfare with a ruthless enemy and the enemy never goes on vacation. His ultimate goal is to weaken your faith and destroy your marriage. This never ending satanic battle against marriage ought to compel the Christian couples to be vigilant and prayerful. We will not have the kind of marriage that God intents us to have unless we are willing to fight for it and pay the price of vigilance. It is incumbent on us as Christians to be aware of the work of the devil who is bent on destroying humanity. Marriage partners must remain on the alert and be sensitive:

"Be sober, be vigilant; because your adversary the devil walks about like a roaring lion, seeking whom he may devour" (1 Peter 5:8).

In order to serve God fully, you need to be free Satanic bondages and personal bondages. To avoid being useless in our lives and ineffective in our marriage, we need to watch and pray (Mark 13:33). We also need to grow spiritually. Spiritual growth will result in victorious living. It will lead to spiritual power and once you are empowered, you will cease being dominated by circumstances and harassed by the devil.[3]

We have at our disposal Jesus Christ as our greatest ally and the Holy Spirit as our greatest helper. As we avail ourselves of the resources that God has provided, we enjoy a victorious marriage and our victory over the enemy is guaranteed. More information about the devil and our spiritual warfare can be found in the books.[4-10]

NOTES

1   M. N. O. Sadiku, *Choosing the Best: Living for What Really Matters*. Bloomington, IN: AuthorHouse, 2012.

2   L. Comes, *Six Lies the Devil Uses to Destroy Marriages*. Houston, TX: Lakewood Church, 1988.

3   M. Atunrase, *7 Realities the Devil Doesn't Want You to Know*. Morrisville, PA: Molat Publishers, 2016, p. 68.

4   R. Joyner, *Overcoming Evil in the Last Days: Exposing Satan's Three Most Powerful Evil Strongholds: Racism, Witchcraft, and the Religious Spirit*. Destiny Image, 2022.

5   K. DeGraw, *Discerning and Destroying the Works of Satan: Your Deliverance Guide to Total Freedom*. Destiny Image Publishers, 2018.

6   Q. Sherrer and R. Garlock, *A Woman's Guide to Spiritual Warfare: How to Protect Your Home, Family and Friends from Spiritual Darkness*. Baker Publishing Group, 2017.

7   C. Trimm, *The Art of War for Spiritual Battle: Essential Tactics and Strategies for Spiritual Warfare*. Charisma House, 2010.

8   T. Evans, Victory in Spiritual Warfare: Outfitting Yourself for the Battle. Harvest House Publishers, 2011.

9   M.I. Bubeck, *The Adversary: The Christian Versus Demon Activity*. Moody Publishers, 2013.

10   T. Olayeri, *Dangerous Prayer That Makes Satan Flee and Surrender Your Possession: Powerful Prayer that Makes Satan Helpless*. Independently Published, 2020.

CHAPTER 6

IRRESPONSIBILITY

"Marriage is another name for responsibilities. If you have sense of responsibility, the purpose of your successful martial will be achieved."
— Anonymous

Although we have free will to make choices as we deem fit, we are morally responsible for those choices in the sense involving deserved blame and praise, punishment and reward. Failure to accept responsibility for own actions is irresponsibility. It is sad but true that most marriages go through a crisis of irresponsibility.

Being in a relationship with someone or marrying someone is a huge responsibility. We all have heard the saying that marriages are made in heaven and celebrated on earth. This is only true when husband and wife jointly work together in a responsible manner and take responsibility of taking care of each other. Only then can they experience a foretaste of heaven on earth.

For a marriage to thrive, you need the ingredients of love, freedom, and responsibility. When two partners are free to disagree, they are free to love. When they are not free, they live in fear, and love dies: "Perfect love drives out fear" (1 John 4:18). Married couples are accountable for their own behavior. In marriage, accountability is answerability. It involves the expectation of account-giving behavior. It is the acknowledgment and assumption of responsibility for actions one takes. It is described as an account-giving relationship husband and wife. Without responsibility and accountability, freedom is in danger of degenerating into mere arbitrariness.

Marital commitment is morally binding, and suggests that husband

and wife act in such a way that minimizes the adverse effect on the other spouse. Married couples can be victorious over great odds when they are willing to make the necessary adjustments and take responsibility for their marriage.

Before we discuss about your marital responsibilities and duties, it may be proper to discuss your marital rights and the causes of irresponsible behaviors. Then we discuss different levels at which married couples discharge their responsibilities: domestic, financial, and spiritual.

MARTIAL RIGHTS

Although marital rights vary from state to state, most states recognize the following spousal rights:[1]

- ability to open joint bank accounts
- ability to file joint federal and state tax returns
- right to receive family rate on health, car and/or liability insurance
- right to inherit spouse's property upon death
- right to sue for spouse's wrongful death
- right to receive spouse's Social Security, pension, worker's compensation, or disability benefits.

In addition, marriage entitles you to a share of all marital property accrued by your spouse during the marriage. Marriage brings financial, legal, social and spiritual benefits as well as duties and responsibilities.

One of the key benefits of marriage is that each partner can each do what he or she is best at and reap the benefits of specialization. God has designed us to be free beings and He does not want us enslaved by each other.

There are certain obligations and responsibilities that come with marital rights. We will discuss them in this chapter.

CAUSES OF IRRESPONSIBILITY

The law of responsibility in marriage states that: A husband and wife are responsible to each other, but not for each other (Galatians 6:2,5).

Irresponsibility occurs when the law of responsibility is not obeyed. An irresponsible husband will neglect his responsibility to love his wife. He may become selfish or inconsiderate.

Our first father, Adam, told God, "Eve made me do it." Eve told God, "The serpent made me do it." Blame-shifting, excuse-making, and irresponsibility are built into our DNA.

Although experts disagree as to what constitute an irresponsible behavior, we all can see it when irresponsibility manifests itself. Here are the ways husband and wife demonstrate irresponsibility at home.

1.   *Lack of domestic support:* Shirking your responsibilities can cause your spouse to feel resentful or create power imbalance in your marriage. Most wives complain that their top source of stress is that their husbands do not want to do their share of chores. When the wife works full time and still ends up doing most of the housework and child care, she resents her husbands' lack of support. If you are endlessly fighting over household responsibilities and roles, your relationship begins to feel adversarial. Figure 1 shows how a wife confronts her irresponsible husband.

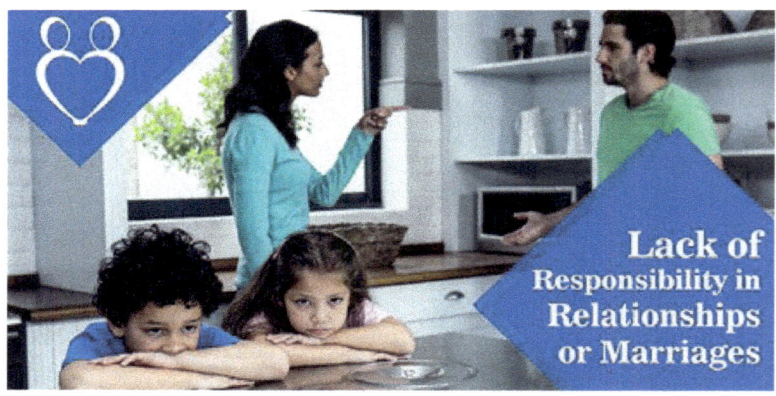

Figure 1 A wife confronts her irresponsible husband.

Source: "Lack of responsibility in relationships or marriages,"

https://saralvaastu.com/lack-of-responsibility-in-relationships-marriages/

2.   *Domestic violence:* Violence is designed to overpower an individual and keep the person in fear of the other. This may take physical, emotional, or sexual abuse.[2] Physical abuse may cause pain,

injury, or bodily harm. Emotional abuse or psychological abuse threatens, intimidates, dehumanizes or undermines self-worth of the victim. Sexual abuse is as any attempt to obtain sexual acts or advances. Any form of abuse is improper in the marriage relationship because a marriage cannot thrive when abuse exists, whether it is physical, emotional, or sexual.

3.   *Addiction:* Alcohol and drug addiction can be linked to domestic violence. Addiction affects millions of Americans each year. A couple may be facing serious problems such as gambling, alcoholism, neglect, workaholic tendencies, poor communication, etc. Unless the husband and wife take responsibility and change their counterproductive behaviors, they will continue in a vicious cycle. Both the abuser and the abused should seek help. There are treatment centers available all over the US that can to help improve your overall quality of life.

4.   *Infidelity:* Infidelity is cheating on a spouse or leaving spouse for another partner. Extramarital sex is a major problem in marriage which can lead to divorce. The solution to infidelity is contentment and self-control. The Bible encourages us to drink from our own well and share our life with only our spouse (Proverbs 5:15). "Don't lust for her beauty. Don't let her coy glances seduce you. For a prostitute will bring you to poverty, but sleeping with another man's wife will cost you your life. For the woman's jealous husband will be furious, and he will show no mercy when he takes revenge" (Proverbs 6:25,26,34, NLT). If your wife does not satisfy your sexual needs, you should discuss it with her. Leaving her for another woman does not show integrity; it only shows an unwillingness to take responsibility for your own happiness. In addition to contentment, we also need self-control, which is one of the nine fruits of the Spirit (Galatians 5:23). Definitely, self-control serves love, not selfishness.

5.   *Wrong Priorities:* Maintaining the proper priority is a constant struggle in many homes. Letting our priorities for our marriage get out of order can lead to acts of irresponsibility. Our priority list in our marriage should go in the following order:[3]

   1.   God

   2.   Family – spouse and children

   3.   Others – job, ministry

These should dictate our levels of commitment.

6.   *Financial Debt:* It is well known fact that marital debt can significantly affect a marriage. Not having enough money to adequately support your family can do great havoc on your emotional and physical well-being. For example, you may lose your job, become pregnant, get sick, become disabled, etc. This can cause your marital debt to increase. It is irresponsible to charge that item on your credit card when you know you will not be able to pay off the bill at the end of the month. Debt can make you to be angry and cause depression.[4] This is why the Bible says, "Owe no man anything, but love one another" (Romans 13:8, KJV). It also says, "The rich rule over the poor, and the borrower is servant to the lender" (Proverbs 22:7, NIV).

7.   *Bad choices:* Other irresponsible actions include stealing, gambling, having cars or houses you cannot afford, and having too many children you cannot financially support their college education. These bad choices can put a lot of stress on your marriage. It is grossly irresponsible not to cut your cloth according to your size. The majority of children raised by irresponsible parents are negatively affected in terms of their academic performance and social functioning. A spouse who is irresponsible and disorganized (misplacing bills and other important personal documents in the house) can make the life of the other partner difficult and miserable. A spouse's irresponsible behavior is a common cause of marital break ups.

Irresponsibility should not be tolerated in marriage. Your marriage can be transformed from irresponsible to mutually responsible one. We will now discuss different ways by which married couples discharge their responsibilities: domestic, financial, and spiritual.

DOMESTIC RESPONSIBILITY

Domestic responsibilities are a time bomb in most homes. Sharing household chores ranks high on issues affecting marriages. The general stereotype was that men do not need help and can handle situations on their own, whereas women were perceived as weaker than men. The women's liberation movement has helped change these stereotypes. God never regarded women as second-class citizens. His Word clearly teaches that we are all equally His children and are of equal value (Galatians 3:28). We discuss domestic responsibility in this section along the following concepts: division of labor, understanding, communication, and shared responsibility.

1.   *Division of Labor:* Several decades ago, the division of labor between husband and wife was clear: he should go to work and earn money, while she should stay at home, cook, clean, and raise the children. This is the traditional model. Things have changed. Today our society has redefined the duties and responsibilities of men and women in society and in the home. More and more women are committed to work outside of the home.

Household work can be categorized into three activities:[5] (1) household maintenance, (2) household chores (e.g., meal preparation, cleaning, outdoor work), (3) childcare. Husband and wife must work together as a team and avoid the 50-50 split. There must be no his work or her work. It is your home, so it is your work. A household will run more smoothly and efficiently if people are allowed to do what they are best at. If you have kids, you should involve them with chores as soon as they are able.

2.   *Understanding:* A fair and satisfactory plan for sharing up household chores begins with mutual understanding. A solid understanding of each other goes a long way in producing happy marriages. To minimize conflict and build healthy lasting relationship, it is important that husband and wife have a clear understanding of how they should relate and what their needs are. Be sensitive to your spouse's natural feelings and tendencies. Rather than fighting against his or her nature, use it to your advantage.

3.   *Communication:* You need to talk about these things openly and honestly. As a team, you should feel free to discuss the differences and aim for reaching consensus. You both live in the home. Therefore, you should both have a say. Before you split chores, agree on what they are: cooking, vacuuming, washing, keeping records or doing the finances, mowing the lawn, taking out the trash, ironing the clothes, cleaning the house, making the bed, etc. Instead of dividing up chores 50-50 or along stereotypical lines, things may work best when you assign the responsibility to the person who is most passionate about that task. Once you have discussed the responsibilities and expectations, your spouse should be able to hold you accountable for performing your duty. If after discussion, your mate fails to do his share of the household chores, keep in mind that you cannot change your spouse. You should consider hiring some outside help or house

cleaner.

4. *Shared responsibility:* As a couple you are on the same team. You should divide household or domestic responsibilities in a way that honors each other. Thriving couples should work together to manage everyday responsibilities. They must reach a consensus and divide household chores fairly as equal partners. Although chores need to be done, but they do not need to be allowed to cause a problem in your home. A Christian couple must not plan based on what other people think. They must seek a plan that preserves fairness and equity in the way they divide household tasks and responsibilities. This will make both spouses happy. Figure 2 shows a family where domestic responsibility is being shared among all family members.

Figure 2 Sharing domestic responsibility by all family members.

Source: "Children helping parents with household chores in kitchen,"

https://stock.adobe.com/fr/images/children-helping-parents-with-household-chores-in-kitchen/179975172

Money plays a role in argument and conflicts between married couples. Instead of the following the traditional model, it is better that you do what works for your marriage and split your financial responsibilities accordingly.

As the husband, a way to demonstrate financial responsibility to your family is to provide for it. As the head of the home, it is your responsibility to meet the material needs of the family. Paul wrote, "But if anyone does not provide for his own, and especially for those of his household, he has denied the faith, and is worse than an unbeliever."

(1 Timothy 5:8).

Since money matters can be emotional and uncomfortable in marriages, it is important to develop strong communication skills that will help openness. Make sure you have short- and long-term goals and you make a plan to reach them. Be willing to address each area of your financial commitment: budget, investment, insurance, and credit cards.

SPIRITUAL RESPONSIBILITY

Too often we consider marriage a social custom and ignore its spiritual dimension. Marriage is a permanent, spiritual union of two personalities under God's law. As Cecil Myers rightly said, "Successful marriage is always a triangle: a man, a woman, and God." The Biblical order of a Christian family is shown in Figure 3.

Figure 3 The Biblical order of a Christian family.

Couples should be willing to take spiritual responsibility for their marriage and do what is necessary to sustain it. A good understanding of your spiritual responsibility or duties, as clearly defined in the Bible, can blend married couples together and produce happy homes.

1. *Duties of the Husband:* The duties of the husband include:[6]

    •   To leave his family and cleave to his wife (Genesis. 2:23,24; Ephesians 5:31).

    •   To be happy with her (Proverbs 5:18)

    •   Not to put her away (I Corinthians 7:11).

    •   To love her as Christ loved the Church (Ephesians 5:25).

    •   To dwell with her according to knowledge (I Peter 3:7).

    •   To fulfill her needs (to feed her, dress her, provide a shelter for her, etc.)

    •   To provide for the family (I Timothy 5:8).

Someone has said, "Marriages may be made in heaven, but man is responsible for the maintenance work." As a man, be a leader, a lover, and servant of your home. You achieve this by modeling godly character, by praying with your wife, and by looking for ways to encourage her spiritually. Love your wife unconditionally (Ephesians 5:25). Show that you love her in words and in actions. Serve your wife by understanding her needs and making efforts to meet them. Understand her language of love and be her confidant.[7]

2. *Duties of the Wife:* The duties of the wife include:[6]

    •   To honor her husband (Esther. 1:20)

    •   To manage the house well (Proverbs 31:27)

    •   To be a helper to her husband (Genesis 2:18)

    •   To respect her husband (Ephesians 5:33)

    •   To be submissive to his leadership and not usurp authority over him) (Ephesians 5:22; I Timothy 2:12)

    •   To be gracious, not slanderous, sober, faithful, and patient (1 Timothy 3:11)

    •   To love her husband and children (Titus 2:4)

- To make herself attractive to him.

As Frederick Sampson rightly said, "God did not create woman to be a competitor but to be a companion." A woman's primary responsibility in marriage is attendance to the needs of her husband. She must respect, honor, and appreciate her husband. Submit to the leadership of your husband and be willing to meet his needs. As you voluntarily submit to him, you are completing him and helping him fulfill his responsibilities and become the man, the husband, and the leader God intended him to be. You are like a thermostat that controls the emotional climate of the house. You may need to "speak the truth in love" to him at times. But do not step into Holy Spirit territory. Be his prayer partner, not his Holy Spirit.

TIME MANAGEMENT

Time management is crucial to the success of your marriage and it is part of your responsibility. Every individual, whether a student, professional, manager, entrepreneur or home-maker, has limited time available to do things. We all have 24 hours a day and 168 hours in every week. How do you spend yours? Why do some people seem to achieve more with their time than others? The answer: good time management. Time is the most precious thing in this world, even more than money. Time management is the process of organizing how much time you devote to specific activities in order to maximize productivity, efficiency, and success. It is a systematic process of organizing and planning how to divide your time into different activities. It is also the ability to use your time productively and efficiently. Proper time management offers countless benefits such as improved work-life balance and a more efficient professional life.[8] Work-life balance is vital in a marriage because it helps to prevent stress and tension between spouses. Like money, time is both valuable and limited. It must be protected, used wisely and effectively. As shown in Figure 4, time is the most precious thing in this world. Time management is making the most out of time.

Figure 4 Time is the most precious thing in the world.

Source: "Time management skills– frequently asked questions,"

https://strategiesforinfluence.com/time-management-skills/

Marriage requires a significant investment of time and energy from both spouses. A successful marriage involves spending quality time with each other and engaging in shared activities. Without proper time management, the demands of work, household chores, and other responsibilities can quickly become overwhelming, leaving little time for relationship. We have seen a marriage in which the husband and wife are so busy with things and they never seem to have time for each other.[9] This is an irresponsible time management. It is also poor time management if you do not have time with God in form of regular devotion. If you are guilty of this, then the following seven tips should be helpful:

- Identify your priorities
- Share responsibilities and the chores
- Use technology to your advantage
- Have time to communicate with each other
- Schedule a day of rest
- Learn when to say no
- Pray together regularly

CONCLUSION

A healthy marriage results when two people work together to make their marriage work and are determined to tackle the problems that threaten it. As married couple, do not let your domestic responsibilities prevent you from meeting each other's most important emotional needs. A marriage thrives when husband and wife are responsible. Your life is your responsibility. Stop blaming others like Adam and Eve. So take responsibility for your own actions.

NOTES

1   K. Otterstrom, "Rights and responsibilities of a married person,"

https://www.lawyers.com/legal-info/family-law/matrimonial-law/rights-and-responsibilities-of-a-married-person.html

2   "Domestic violence," Wikipedia, the free encyclopedia

https://en.wikipedia.org/wiki/Domestic_violence

3   M. N. O. Sadiku and J. O. Sadiku, Secrets of Successful Marriages. Bloomington, IN: iUniverse, 2nd edition, 2022, p. 168.

4   "The emotional effects of marital debt,"

http://relationshipcounselingcenter.net/emotional-effects-marital-debt/

5   W. Klein, C. Izquierdo, and T. N. Bradbury, "The difference between a happy marriage and miserable one: Chores," March 2015,

https://www.theatlantic.com/sexes/archive/2013/03/the-difference-between-a-happy-marriage-and-miserable-one-chores/273615/

6   "Marriage and responsibility,"

http://www.biblicalfulfillment.org/id61.html

7   J. Karina, "Roles and responsibilities in marriage,"

http://www.jenniekarina.co.ke/roles-and-responsibilities-in-marriage/

8   M. N. O. Sadiku, C. M. M. Kotteti, and J. O. Sadiku, "Time management 101," to appear.

9   "The importance of managing and balancing your time in marriage,"

https://ultimateintimacy.com/the-importance-of-managing-and-balancing-your-time-in-marriage/

CHAPTER 7

MIXED FAITH

"Do not be misdated with unbelievers. For what partnership have righteousness and iniquity? Or what fellowship has light with darkness?"
(2 Corinthians 6:14).

The three major influences on our lives are culture, religion, and education. Religion plays a variety of roles in our daily lives. Therefore, mixed faith is a major enemy of marriages because it always causes social and marital frictions. Differences in faith between spouse leads unnecessary conflicts. I say this partly from experience because my dad was a Christian, while my mom was a Muslim. Both my dad and mom were Muslims originally. When my dad got converted to Christianity in 1965, everyone in the polygamous family was converted except my mom. She remained a Muslim until she died in 2009.

Interfaith (or mixed-faith) marriage (or religious intermarriage) refers to marriage between partners professing different religions.[1] This kind of marriage was uncommon until the modern age. Today, many people marry across religious lines. Mixed-faith marriages are made up of married couples who are from different religious backgrounds. Such marriages are becoming common in the US as they represent close to half of all marriages in the past 10 years. Interfaith marriage differs from interracial and inter-ethnic marriage because spouses in an interfaith marriage may share the same race or ethnicity.

The intermarriage of Christians and Muslims, Catholics and Protestants, Jews and gentiles, Hindus and Mormons, or evangelicals and non-evangelicals is increasing significantly. However, such interfaith marriages usually come with a heavy price. Compared with same-faith unions, interfaith couples tend to be unhappy and mixed-faith marriages often end in tears.

MIXED FAITH WEDDING

A mixed faith wedding is a celebration where a couple with two different religious backgrounds combine both of their religious traditions throughout their wedding. Such a wedding ceremony presents some unique challenges and can be complex. The challenges include possible questions from family members, who will pay for what, which practices to include, and how to choose an officiant. To overcome the challenges there must be an open dialogue between you, your partner, and both families. Some couples choose to highlight both of their faiths during their wedding ceremony and leave the reception secular. Since there is not one way to plan a mixed faith wedding ceremony, every ceremony is unique, depending on the couple, their faiths, and their customs. Premarital counseling may or may not be required for an interfaith wedding.[2] A typical interfaith wedding (between a Jew and a Christian) is shown in Figure 1.

Figure 1 A typical interfaith wedding.

Source: "How to successfully mix two religions into one beautiful interfaith wedding ceremony," July 2016,

https://www.smashingtheglass.com/how-to-successfully-mix-two-faiths-into-one-beautiful-wedding-ceremony/

MIXED FAITH MARRIAGE IS FORBIDDEN

The issue of religion can often be the cornerstone of strife in a interfaith union. Shared religious faith is crucial for a successful marriage. If you have fundamentally different spiritual beliefs, this may present an additional challenge in your relationship for an entire lifetime. You will be prevented from sharing a big part of your life with your spouse. This negates much of the bonding that usually comes with same-faith marriages.

Most religions strictly prohibit interfaith unions. Mixed-faith unions are forbidden in Christianity, Islam, and Judaism.

For the sake of compatibility and the upbringing of future children, these world religions forbid mixed marriages. This policy is based on protecting the religion and deterring both man and woman from doing things that jeopardize their faith.

Most Christian denominations forbid interfaith marriage based on 2 Corinthians 6:14 and Deuteronomy 7:3. Ezra asked the people of Israel to divorce their pagan wives and send them away with their children (Ezra 10:2,3). Nehemiah along with the leaders of Israel promised not to let their daughters marry pagans of the land and not to let their sons marry their daughters (Nehemiah 10:30). Jesus taught that you should value and love Him above all other relationships (Luke 14:26). The apostle Paul commands that Christians must "not be unequally yoked with unbelievers" (2 Corinthians 6:14). Avoiding being "unequally yoked" is an excellent biblical advice. Christians should not marry an unbeliever because this violates the believer's union with Christ. We must keep in mind that Christians approach marriage as a covenant, a relationship based on promises and commitment.

For those who embrace a religious outlook on life, faith is a way of life. For those individuals, religion means having a set of values and principles which guide individuals through life. In mixed-faith families, parents come from different faith backgrounds, in any combination between Christian, Hindu, Muslim, and Jew.[3] The diversity of religion may be the source of frequent domestic strife and discord. This could prevent marriage from fulfilling its intended purpose. Mixed-faith marriage contradicts the principle according to which a man and woman constitute a unity of body and spirit in marriage.[4]

King Solomon made a major self-destructive mistake in marriage. He married multiple foreign women who rejected faith in God alone. As wise and powerful as he was, he could not turn those women to God. The women turned him away from God. When he became old, his wives turned his heart away after other gods and God was not pleased with him (1 Kings 11:4).

BENEFITS AND CHALLENGES

Perhaps the major benefit of interfaith marriage is that it potentially promotes religious education, tolerance, and accommodation in the society. It also produces religiously tolerant and abundantly enlightened children. Marrying someone of another faith tended to improve one's view of that faith. The more one knows people of another faith, the more they like them. With time both partners may decide to merge their two faiths and pursue a way of life that they can both share. Love is very strong and can overlook a lot. If romance movies have taught us anything, it is that love conquers all, even for people with different faiths. A mixed-faith couple in loving relationship is shown in Figure 2.

Figure 2 A typical mixed-faith couple.

Source: S. K. Saad, "7 Couples give their best advice on how to be in an interfaith relationship," September 2020,

https://www.cosmopolitan.com/sex-love/a34078016/interfaith-relationships/

However, an interfaith marriage can pose some challenges to the couple, to the children, and to extended families. Being in an interfaith relationship may be a significant source of stress for couples. A power struggle always exists over which religion is better. Theologians and sociologists contend that interfaith marriages weaken the religious commitment of the individuals forming the unions and the commitment of the offspring is low.[5] Interfaith marriages are generally less religious than their same-faith counterparts, they attend religious services less often, pray less frequently, and discuss religious matters with their spouses less frequently. Interfaith couples are often less satisfied than same-faith couples. Religion is often less important to children raised by interfaith couples. When you are in an interfaith marriage, avoiding conflict may require even more effort. Some mixed-faith marriages end in tears and there is evidence that mixed-faith couples have a somewhat higher rate of divorce than do same-faith couples.

Celebrating religious occasions like Hanukkah and Christmas, Passover and Easter, can be uncomfortable for interfaith couples. Such religious festivals or anniversaries, birthdays, wedding ceremonies, and funerals can present some tensions. It is impractical to raise children in two competing sets of beliefs. Interfaith marriages tend to gravitate to Unitarian Universalism and produce dual-faith children.

STRENGTHENING INTERFAITH MARRIAGE

According to Naomi Schaefer Rile,[6] couples tend to have tensions over three things: how to raise your kids, how to spend your time, and how to spend your money. And religion affects all of those things. 1 Corinthians 7:13-16 is one of the few passages that address interfaith marriages.

Unfortunately, interfaith couples often do not know where to turn to get their problems solved. Your two-religion household can be effective and become a blended family if proper care is taken. Here are some tips that can help you enjoy an interfaith marriage.[7]

1.   *Communicate:* Communication is the process by which you let your spouse know about your feelings, thoughts, problems, etc. It is crucial that you have a thorough, open communication with your spouse on a regular basis. Do not bottle up something you feel is wrong. That will cause resentment and lead to other problems. You should create time and opportunities to discuss faith. Frequency of religious discussion in mixed-faith marriage is shown in Figure 3.

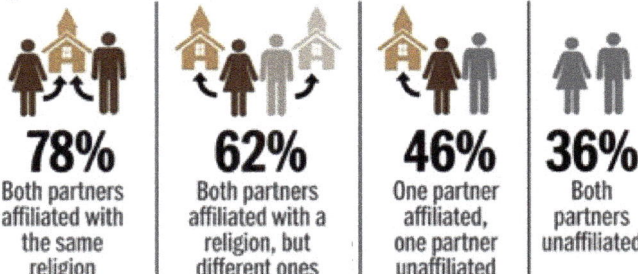

Frequency of religious discussions

Percentage of U.S. adults in the following type of marriage who talk about religion "a lot" or "some" with their spouse

78%	62%	46%	36%
Both partners affiliated with the same religion	Both partners affiliated with a religion, but different ones	One partner affiliated, one partner unaffiliated	Both partners unaffiliated

Figure 3 Frequency of religious discussion in mixed-faith marriage.

Source: K. Dallas, "What couples may not realize about religion and marriage," October 2016,

https://www.deseret.com/2016/10/26/20599051/what-couples-may-not-realize-about-religion-and-marriage

You should discuss what you want your child to encounter. Although a child is capable of integrating the two worldviews of their parents, a child cannot be a Muslim and a Catholic at the same time. Parents must decide which way they will raise their child. It is important to make this tough decision earlier on in the relationship. As long as the married couple have a strong relationship with open communication, they can allow their child to make their own informed choices.[8] There is no universal right way in which "mixed" parents should bring up their "mixed" children.

2.   *Educate yourself:* (This is still part of communication.) It is critically important to teach yourself about your spouse's faith and culture. The more you know about your spouse, the more you grow in your love for him. Participate and be involved in your spouse's rituals and celebrations. Build bridges of understanding between the two of you.

3.   *Be Flexible:* To make your marriage work, you should be willing to give and take. Be willing to compromise in resolving your marital conflicts. Cherish and enjoy your differences. The earlier you work through your differences the better. Doing so will help you navigate the differences for better rather than for worse.

4.   *Don't try to change Your Spouse:* If your partner wants to convert and change faith, let it come from their personal decision Do not force, nag, or give ultimatums. Let love and action do the talking. No one enjoys being criticized for what they believe. Criticizing one another on your faiths can be devastating on your relationship. Respect the beliefs and values of your spouse. Do not allow the enemy to use your faiths to tear you apart.

CONCLUSION

Marriage has changed as the society around it has. We are in the era of interfaith marriage. As couples abandon religious boundaries and traditions, religious intermarriages are becoming common. Globalization and migration have greatly contributed to the recent rise of exogamy or interfaith marriages. Although close experience of another faith may be enlightening, it is also challenging. Christian or not, marriage is very hard for any couple to sustain over a lifetime. Statistics show that more than half of the marriages end up in divorce. If you are in an interfaith marriage, your marriage can not only survive a faith crisis, but it can thrive as deeply satisfying friendships. Your marriage can be both successful and happy if you can do what it takes, as recommended above. Other helpful resources include the books.[9-14]

NOTES

1   R. Cigdem, "Interfaith marriage in comparative perspective," *Acta Orientalia Academiae Scientiarum Hung.*, vol. 68, no. 1, 2015, pp. 59 – 86.

2   C. Johnson, "Everything you need to know about mixed faith wedding ceremonies," August 2022,

https://www.theknot.com/content/interfaith-wedding-questions

3   E. Arweck and E. Nesbitt, "Young people's identity formation in mixed-faith families: Continuity or discontinuity of religious traditions?", *Journal of Contemporary Religion*, vol. 25, no. 1, 2010, pp. 67-87

4   C. Cristellon, "Between sacrament, sin and crime: Mixed marriages and the Roman Church in early modern Europe,"

Gender & History, vol.29. no.3, November 2017, pp. 605–621.

5   L. R. Peterson, "Interfaith marriage and religious commitment among Catholics," *Journal of Marriage and the Family*, vol. 48, no. 4, November 1986, pp. 725-735.

6   N. S. Riley, *'Til Faith Do Us Part': How Interfaith Marriage Is Transforming America*. New York: Oxford University Press, 2013.

7   J. Keen, "Avoiding conflict in an interfaith marriage,"

https://www.kveller.com/article/avoiding-conflict-in-an-interfaith-marriage/

8   E. Arweck and E. Nesbitt, "Religious education in the experience of young people from mixed faith families," *British Journal of Religious Education*, vol. 33, no. 1, 2011, pp.31-45.

9   D. McGowan, *In Faith and In Doubt: How Religious Believers and Nonbelievers Can Create Strong Marriages and Loving Families*. New York: AMACOM, 2014.

10   S. K. Miller, *Being Both: Embracing Two Religions in One Interfaith Family*. Boston, MA: Beacon Press Books, 2013.

11   E. B. Seamon, *Interfaith Marriage in America: The Transformation of Religion and Christianity*. New York: Palgrave Macmillan, 2012.

12   S. Kielsmeier-Cook, *Blessed Are the Nones: Mixed-Faith*

Marriage and My Search for Spiritual Community. IVP, 2020.

13   N. H. Parker, *One Family, Two Views: How to Fortify Your Mixed-Faith Mormon Marriage.* CreateSpace Independent Publishing Platform, 2018

14   N. S. Riley, *'Til Faith Do Us Part: How Interfaith Marriage is Transforming America.* Oxford University Press, 2013.

CHAPTER 8

NAGGING AND CRITICISM

"Better to live in a wilderness than with a nagging and hot-tempered wife"
(Proverbs 21:19).

To nag is to bug or make a big deal out of doing something small. Nagging is endless scolding, complaining, and faultfinding. It may also be regarded as constantly criticizing someone. When you complain about or say something over and over again, then it becomes nagging. Nagging can occur in the workplace or at home.

If you find yourself repeating something to your husband multiple times, you are engaging in nagging behavior. While most women do not like to nag, unless they feel unheard, overworked, or taken-for-granted, nagging indicates trouble in the relationship. Nagging is a disguised form of controlling someone's behavior.

Nagging in a marriage is a common problem. It is poison to a marriage. It is one of the most common relationship complaints couples express. It is never an effective way to communicate your needs or requests. It can be harmful to a relationship and it often produces negative results. It causes vexing and irritation to both partners. It is an enemy of marriages.

Nagging is a form of persistent persuasion that is designed to gain compliance.[1] Nagging is an aggressive, nasty behavior that can stem from unbelief, unmet needs, feeling unheard and unsupported. It is often perceived as criticism and can make others feel inadequate.

Although both men and women nag, nagging is mostly done by women. We have all seen a woman or wife always complaining about things around the home, about her husband, her children, or her job. Women try to get what they want by nagging and criticizing it out of their husband and children. Much of their criticism is well-intentioned. That may be their own way of saying we care and demanding to see a change. Figure 1 shows a typical nagging wife, while Figure 2 depicts a nagging husband.

Figure 1 A nagging wife.

Figure 2 A nagging husband.

King Solomon, the wisest man that ever lived, wrote that is better to sit on a roof and live in a desert than live with a nagging wife (Proverbs 21:9,19). Delilah finally caused Samson's demise by nagging until he revealed the secret of his strength. Satan may use nagging and criticism to do some havoc in your marriage.

This chapter first considers what is wrong with nagging. It then presents ways of stopping or minimizing nagging and criticism in marriage.

WHAT IS WRONG WITH NAGGING

But we all hate nagging. It does not feel like love. Parents are unwittingly, too critical of their children. Parents who nag or overcriticize their children are destroying their fragile self-esteem. Unfortunately, those who nag may not realize that they are nagging. The nagger should understand that there are dangerous consequences for his or her actions. Here are the reasons nagging will not get you what you want in any relationship:[2]

1.   *Resentment:* Because no one likes nagging, nagging will likely generate an angry response from your partner, making them resent you. The more you nag, the less they will respond to your requests.

2.   *Negativity:* When you nag, you find fault in your partner. You are implying what your partner is doing is wrong. Who needs nagging, nit-picking, criticism, and negativity? Though one may feel bad after being criticized, later try to find something helpful about the comment. Begin to see the positive side of things.

3.   *Hostility:* Nagging is a form of criticism and it creates hostility in a relationship. Criticism generally can be valid or unjustified. It is difficult, if not impossible, to feel love and acceptance in a nagging or critical environment. You come home from work thinking of finally getting peace, but what you actually get is war. Figure 3 shows husband and wife that are not happy with each other.

Figure 3 An unhappy couple.

Source: E. Bader, "What dynamics make change so challenging and hard to transcend?"

https://www.couplesinstitute.com/what-dynamics-make-change-so-challenging-and-hard/

4.   *Dominance:* When you nag your partner, you are treating them like you are dominant and what you say needs to happen at all costs. This is an unhealthy approach to forming a long-lasting and meaningful relationship. Remember, you are a partner, not a dictator.

5.   *Lack of Satisfaction:* As they say, "A happy wife, a happy life." A nagging wife is never satisfied with her husband and undermines him at every chance she gets. Her words hurt and humiliate her man. Stress from a nagging wife is a constant irritant a man has to deal with. Both husband and wife are not happy or satisfied.

HOW TO COPE WITH NAGGING

Nagging is persistently annoying or finding fault with your partner. It often takes place when a person is dissatisfied with something. The sole responsibility of the marriage according to Gods blueprint falls on the man. Since nagging can ruin your relationship, you need to know how to cope or deal with it. Here are 10 ways a husband can cope with a nagging wife:[3]

1.   Don't answer back

2.   Try to calm her down or walk away if necessary

3.   Identify your mistake and apologize

4. Pay attention to what she has to say

5. Try to see things from her perspective

6. Discuss your own perspective

7. Negotiate with her

8. Ask her to accept you

9. Reassure her and show affection

10. Talk to a counselor if necessary

Sometimes, it is the husband who is complaining and nagging about something. If a wife is being nagged a lot by her husband, there are certain things she can do to cope. The Bible says that you can win your husband without a word (2 Peter 3:1,2). The following 10 tips will help a wife cope with a nagging husband:[4]

1. Identify the reason behind the nagging

2. Don't react on impulse

3. Be careful of the way you respond

4. Talk to him about how you feel

5. Listen to what he is saying

6. Pay attention to his concern and response

7. Make agreements for things that bother your partner

8. You may tease him and joke about his nagging

9. Put your partner's comments in perspective

10. Consider couples therapy if necessary

HOW TO STOP NAGGING AND CRITICISM

It is quite unhealthy for your marriage to be filled with nagging and criticism. If your spouse is nagging, there are various ways to cope. These ways are discussed in the previous section as short-term solutions. Here we look at long-term solutions or actions you must take to stop nagging and criticism in your marriage and avoid their negative effects. You should take the following actions to stop or minimize nagging and criticism.[5,6]

1. *Just stop Nagging:* It takes two people to nag. If one stops, it is mostly likely that the other too will stop nagging. Asking for the

same thing over and over again does not work. Although nagging may produce a short-term positive result, you cannot nag someone into permanent change. The sooner you stop, the better chance your relationship will have to grow. The person being nagged should stay calm and disengage, if necessary. It is best not to respond immediate but to wait a little before responding. If nagger does not stop, you should feel free to walk away and maintain peace. Joe J. Christensen said, "Few people have ever changed for the better as a result of constant criticism or nagging. If we are not careful, some of what we offer as constructive criticism is actually destructive."

2.   *Communicate:* Communication is one of the things that can make or break a relationship. It has been well said that all behavior is communication and all communication affects behavior. It is the process of creating meaning between people. As a couple, have you talked about the roles each of you should play in your marriage? Set aside time to be with her for daily conversations. Although nagging is not the best way to communicate, she may find it easier to reach you that way. If you have an issue, bring it up once or twice and talk about it. Talk about the issues and make changes to improve your relationship instead of just being annoyed.

3.   *Respect Your Spouse:* There is no better antidote for criticism and nagging than patient and respectful listening. Focus the nagging or criticism on the behavior that needs to change. Pay attention on what your spouse is saying. Make sure that your spouse still feels loved and respected. It is important for your spouse to know that his or her nagging and criticism is harming your spirit.

4.   *Find a Better Time to Criticize:* Criticizing or receiving criticism is very important in any healthy relationship. Criticism is always important for happiness in your relationship and for keeping things in proportion, but it must be done at an appropriate time and place. It must be clear and constructive. Having a constructive criticism or feedback can often be a good thing for a healthy relationship. It is important to strike a good balance between being excessively critical and being totally uncritical. When criticism is not done properly, it will fail to achieve its intended purpose, even although it is well-intentioned. Learning from constructive criticism or feedback allows you to improve. Criticism allows an opportunity to choose peace over conflict.

5.   *Be Understanding:* Through understanding , you can choose to approach your marital problems with patience and compassion. Understand that nobody likes being criticized but, unfortunately it is a fact of life. Put yourself in the spouse's shoes. The best way to understand your spouse's viewpoint is to listen to what they are saying. Accept that you are not perfect. Understand where he or she is really coming from. It is unhealthy to keep your emotions bottled up. At an appropriate time, voice your feelings.

6.   *Compromise:* Marital relationship function best on give and take. You cannot change someone else, but you can only change yourself. Find a common ground. When compromising on something, be sure neither of you are trying to attain something unrealistic. When you show that you are willing to change or help, your partner will be willing to do that same. You may find that spending quality time with her at least once a week may stop the nagging.

7.   *Go to counseling:* If after you have tried everything and you cannot fix the problem, you may want to seek outside help. Do not be shy to seek help from a family friend, your pastor, a mentor, or a professional counselor. You should not deal with big problems in marriage all by yourself. Counseling can afford you the privilege to learn new ways to communicate and reach an agreement. It is recommended that you both attend the counseling so that you can work on solving the problem together.

CONCLUSION

Nagging is something that most of us do and may not even realize it. It is a subtle enemy of your marriage.

It is not conducive to good relationships, whether it is a father prodding a child or a wife prodding her husband. Pray to God about it. Ask the Holy Spirit to help you change. Nagging spirit, a form of domestic criticism, is so ugly that we must keep it out of our homes. Learn to overlook little, little inconsequential things. Don't major in minors. It is important that you find ways to resolve your marital conflicts, stop nagging, and start enjoying your marriage again. Incredible marriages are possible if we eliminate nagging and criticism in our marriages.

NOTES

1   "Nagging," *Wikipedia*, the free encyclopedia

https://en.wikipedia.org/wiki/Nagging

2   C. Truffo, "Why nagging won't get you what you want,"

https://www.theravive.com/today/post/why-nagging-wont-get-you-what-you-want-0000237.aspx

3   "12 Smart and easy ways to deal with a nagging wife,"

https://www.bonobology.com/deal-nagging-wife/

4   O. Surtees, "How to deal with a nagging husband (9 best ways)," February 2023,

https://hernorm.com/nagging-husband/

5   "Criticism," *Wikipedia*, the free encyclopedia

https://en.wikipedia.org/wiki/Criticism

6   "How to deal with criticism,"

https://www.wikihow.com/Deal-With-Criticism

CHAPTER 9

INFIDELITY

"Flee from sexual immorality. All other sins a person commits are outside the body, but whoever sins sexually, sins against their own body"
(1 Corinthians 6:18).

Infidelity is also known as cheating, adultery, unfaithfulness, betrayal, or disloyalty. It is breaking a promise to remain faithful to a sexual partner. The promise may be the marriage vows made between lovers in the presence of many witnesses. It is being unfaithful to your spouse. Although both women and men commit fidelity, men appear to be more prone to affairs. A man and a woman committing adultery are shown in Figure 1.

Figure 1 A man and a woman committing adultery.

Source: H. Gornbein, "14 Most common causes of infidelity in a marriage," April 2021, https://www.divorcemag.com/blog/most-common-causes-of-infidelity-in-a-marriage

Infidelity takes place in 20 to 25% of all marriages. According to one source, 36 percent of men and women admit to having an affair with a coworker and 35 percent of men and women admit to cheating while on a business trip. Figure 2 shows that married men are more likely to cheat than married women.

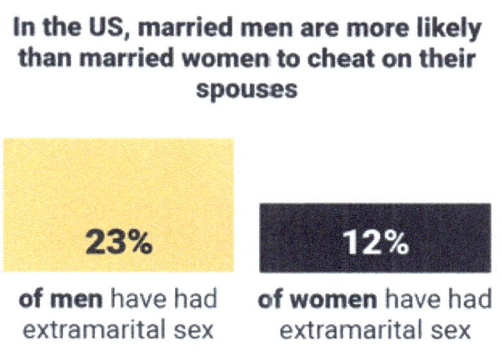

Figure 2 Married men are more likely to cheat than married women.

Source: Sebastian, "Infidelity statistics 2023: Do men or women cheat more?" August 2023,

https://relationshipsadvice.co/cheating-statistics/

Infidelity is a violation of a couple's sexual exclusivity expectations. This violation results in feelings of rage, betrayal, jealousy, and rivalry. Infidelity is threatening and devastating to marriage. It is regarded as a betrayal and it destroys the fabric of a relationship which is difficult to repair. The betrayal of the marital exclusivity is done through lies and deception - the two main features of adultery.

Today, infidelity is regarded as the most important reason of divorces. According to Jesus, sexual immorality is the only ground for divorce (Matthew 5:32). Infidelity or sexual immorality is a significant problem that seriously affects marriage. Therefore, we should see infidelity as an enemy of marriage. Although infidelity can be a problem in dating relationships,[1] in this chapter, we restrict it to marital relationship.

SIGNS OF INFIDELITY

There is almost nothing that can destroy a marital relationship more quickly than infidelity. Here are some signs that you partner may be cheating:[2,3]

1. Your gut says something is up.

2. They become inseparable with their computer/mobile phones

3. You keep hearing about this "friend"

4. They are no longer there for you

5. You are usually less attractive to them

6. They stopped liking you as a person

7. There is more emotional distance than there used to be.

8. They are gone more often than they used to be.

9. They are making big cash withdrawals.

10. You start catching your partner in little white lies.

11. They get defensive

12. They are hiding their phone from you

CAUSES OF INFIDELITY

Infidelity is one of the worst things that can happen to a relationship. It is one of the factors that can destroy a marriage. Infidelity is caused mainly by a number of factors, including lack of satisfaction, workplace temptation, seeking pleasure, pornography, and cybersex.

1. *Lack of satisfaction:* Men are more likely to engage in extramarital sex if they are unsatisfied sexually, while women are more likely to engage in extramarital sex if they are unsatisfied emotionally. For women, relationship dissatisfaction is the number one reason for infidelity, whereas for men it is lack of communication and sexual incompatibility.[4]

2. *Workplace:* As the number of women in the workforce increases, one would expect the likelihood of infidelity will increase. Workplace interaction between men and women can lead to marital infidelity.[5] The increase in working hours, after work meetings, and a need to work out of town for prolonged periods of time may expose a worker to temptation on infidelity. Married women are less likely

to have an affair with co-workers. Although companies cannot ban adultery, they can promote zero tolerance for sexual harassment.

3.   *Pleasure:* Humans are promiscuous and depraved. People get involved in infidelity because of the pleasure, thrill, or excitement associated with sex. Like any other sin, sexual affair is sweet. Although affairs can be incredibly sexy, compelling, addictive and sweet, most of them end and the thrill wears off. Reality will set in and infatuation will fade. Most of us underestimate the strength of attraction as compared to the strength of our self-control. Like the man in Figure 3, some men cannot resist the temptation of looking at an attractive woman.

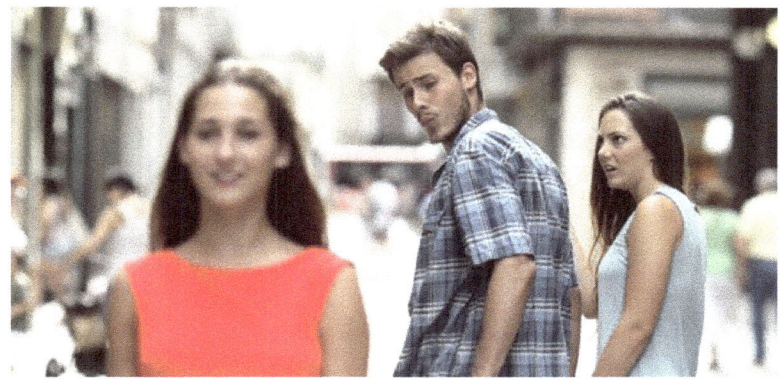

Figure 3 A man reacting to an attractive alternative.

Source: A. Pawlowski, "What helps a person stay faithful? 2 behaviors may be key," September 2018,

https://www.euronews.com/culture/2013/09/12/how-stay-faithful-prevent-infidelity-behaviors-help-t137265

4.   *Pornography:* Pornography (or porn) consists of sexually explicit material intended to sexually arouse one who views it. It also comes in the forms of magazines, movies, TV shows, and romantic novels, which glamorize sexual affairs. These media promote attractive, near naked models. Today porn is readily available at the click of a button by anyone who has Internet connection.[6]

5.   *Internet:* The use of smart phones and the Internet have provided us with convenient media to engage in interactions outside of the primary relationship. The proliferation of sex chat rooms and

dating apps has enabled people to engage in acts of infidelity on and off the Internet. The Internet allows users to hide their identity. Some believe that if a partner engages in cybersex (sexual relationship initiated by an online contact) this constitutes infidelity. Cybersex can become addictive and needs to be addressed. Social media makes it easy to exchange sexy pictures with an illicit lover.

Other causes of infidelity include unhappy marriages, lack of love/affection, longing for variety of sexual experiences, revenge, appearance, and illness of the faithful partner. Be observant and notice if any of these causes occur in your marriage. Observe if your partner acts suspiciously when phoning or texting. Changes in his/her behavior and appearance may indicate unfaithfulness.

EFFECTS OF INFIDELITY

With infidelity come consequences. It has rocked many marriages. It affects many people. After the unfaithful partner is found out, feelings of shame, guilt, despair, betrayal, and confusion are evident. The betrayed partner feels disappointed and grieves. Even a single infidelity event can lead to untold harm and conflict.

1.   *Lack of Interest In Sex:* His sexual interest with you may have waned since he is getting his sexual satisfaction elsewhere. He becomes emotionally distant, withdrawn or depressed. The unfaithful spouse became angry and critical. He changes behavior.

2.   *Jealousy:* Infidelity is a violation of a couple's sexual exclusivity expectations. This violation results in feelings of rage, betrayal, jealousy, and rivalry. Jealousy is a romantic partner's negative reaction to the sexual involvement of the partner with someone else. The manifestation of jealousy differs for men and women. Women feel upset when their husband invests resources in another woman. Men particularly fear that their mate will have sex with someone else.[7] According to the Bible, "The man who commits adultery is an utter fool, for he destroys himself. For the woman's jealous husband will be furious, and he will show no mercy when he takes revenge" (Proverbs 6:32,34).

3.   *Punishment:* While infidelity is not regarded as a criminal offense in Europe and America, it is criminalized in many countries in Africa, Asia, and Middle East. Most cultures have ways of inflicting

punishment on cheaters. In the US penalties for adultery range from life imprisonment in Michigan, to a $10 fine in Maryland or class 1 felony in Wisconsin.[4] The wise man said, "Sleeping with another man's wife will cost you your life" (Proverbs 6:26).

4.   *Disobedience:* While adultery is cheating on your spouse, it is also disobeying God. It is violating the sixth commandment: "You shall not commit adultery" (Exodus 20:14). "Marriage should be honored by all, and the marriage bed kept pure, for God will judge the adulterer and all the sexually immoral" (Hebrews 13:4).

5.   *Losses:* Some people regard the aftermath of infidelity as worse than losing their partner through death. This is based on the fact that relationships survive after death, but do not always survive after infidelity. The losses experienced in infidelity include:[8]

- Loss of trust
- Loss of security
- Loss of hope/dreams
- Loss of faith
- Loss of intimacy and affection
- Loss of self esteem
- Loss of identity
- Loss of feeling special
- Loss of self-respect

Infidelity can impair the trust, security, connection, and intimacy level within couples.[9]

6.   *Divorce:* Divorce may result from infidelity, but infidelity need not result in divorce. We must keep in mind that divorce often creates more problems than it solves. It is more problematic if children are involved. Rather than dissolving the marriage, the affair could be used as a catalyst for positive changes in the marriage.

Other effects include family instability, violence, abuse, and health problems. A wife in Figure 4 feels disappointed.

Figure 4 A disappointed wife.

Source: L. Brown, "How can you tell if your partner has cheated? Here are 16 signs," https://ideapod.com/cheating-sleeping-someone-else-9-signs-partner-guilty/

PREVENTING INFIDELITY

Infidelity is common in the United States and other parts of the world. Preventing infidelity is better than repairing after an affair. Many divorces could have been avoided if couple took some preventing measures. Some people fall into having an affair simply because they feel that they are not appreciated at home. The following tips will help from falling into the trap of infidelity:[10]

1.   *Commitment to Meeting Needs:* Some people fall into having an affair simply because they feel that they are not appreciated at home. Some men confess that they are not having enough sex with their wife. Women can do without sex for years, but men cannot do without it for weeks. Most women do not understand this. To prevent infidelity, a woman should make sure she satisfies her husband very well in this area. Dress well to sexually attract your husband and showcase your beauty from time to time. Having date nights with your partner is a must. Happy couples enjoy each other's company. Take interest in what your partner enjoys and try doing it with them. If people continued to consciously keep "chasing" their spouse, affairs and divorces could be avoided.

2.   *Avoid Temptation:* A wife should not have an open door of temptation for their husband. Ordinary house maid, female friends of the wives, female relatives of the wife, and female workers at home

can be a source of temptation to the husband. A couple must set boundaries to prevent the husband from falling into temptation with these close acquaintances of the wife. The last thing you want to do is find yourself alone with a member of the opposite sex.

3.   *Keep Your Vow:* Infidelity is betraying your spouse and breaking your marriage vows. The betrayal of a partner in a marriage is one of the most traumatizing events that can happen to anyone. It sometimes destroys everything that a couple has built over the years. In many cases, love is shattered, trust is broken, families are torn apart, and both spouses and their children suffer the pain. When you consider the gain and the loss, infidelity is not worth it. Make up your mind not to betray your spouse and be responsible. Be a good and faithful partner.

4.   *Avoid Comparison:* One easy way to fall into the trap of infidelity is to keep comparing one's partner to another person, or comparing one's marriage with another marriage. For example, social media bombards us with information about others and forces us to compare them with our own spouse. It is wise to block certain individuals you find yourself comparing your spouse.

5.   *Guard Your Heart:* Cheating is ultimately a choice one is given under some circumstance. It usually begins in the heart and eventually leads to emotional heartbreak. Therefore, you must guard your heart and not play with the Satan when he brings temptation. Proverbs 4:23 says, "Guard your heart above all else, or it determines the course of your life" (NLT). You must hold yourself to a higher standard, which is the Word of God. Use yourself as a standard for other people to emulate. Ephesians 5:3 says, "But among you there must not be even a hint of sexual immorality, or of any kind of impurity, or of greed, because these are improper for God's holy people." Infidelity is toxic to your spiritual wellbeing. It sin against God and your spouse. You cannot escape God's judgment soon or later. "Sleeping with another man's wife will cost you your life" (Proverbs 6:26, NLT).

OVERCOMING INFIDELITY

Just as loving moments are shared together, couples must be prepared to share negative experience. This is part of their commitment to one another: "for better, for worse." Overcoming the devastation of infidelity is not easy, but it can be done. If you suspect that your partner may be cheating, both of you should work as a team and take the following actions.

1.   *Confess:* Since infidelity is a sin against God and your partner, you need to confess it and ask for their forgiveness. The Bibles asks us to flee sexual immorality and from any appearance of evil (1 Corinthians 6:18). As part of confession, the unfaithful partner should disclose all of the steps leading to their affair. The person must be willing to make a major commitment and regain their spouse's trust.[11]

2.   *Forgive:* The infidel or unfaithful should seek forgiveness of the betrayed spouse. This involves restoration and making a deeper commitment to honor and love their spouse. The betrayed spouse should be willing to forgive the unfaithful spouse. We all make mistakes and we all need forgiveness. Forgiveness lightens up and is freeing. Love begins to flow again.

3.   *Address the issues:* Statistics shows that women initiate about 75% of all divorces. But most people choose not to divorce but to stay in their marriages after infidelity. Divorce is not the solution, especially when the cheating spouse is remorseful and willing to change. The solution is to find out the issues that caused the infidelity and find ways to address them. It takes time, effort, and hard work to confront all the issues and mend the marriage.[12]

4.   *Seek Help:* It is expedient to get professional help or talk to friends or relatives who will be less judgmental. Experienced couple therapists deal with the issue of infidelity on a regular basis in their clinical practices. With proper professional counseling, couples stand a good chance of overcoming the trauma of infidelity/affair.

CONCLUSION

Infidelity is an event that results in the most damage to a marriage. It can disrupt even so-called happy marriages. If left unchecked, infidelity can cause harm to a marriage. The good news is that you can recover your marriage, but it takes time and teamwork to heal from infidelity.

If your marriage is in need of restoration right now, pray that God will intervene, guide, and give you wisdom. Remove the option of divorce, forgive, and reconcile. God hates divorce (Malachi 2:16) and loves those who obey Him by not divorcing their spouse. More information on infidelity can be found in the books.[13-15]

NOTES

1   R. D. McAnulty and J. M. Brineman, "Infidelity in dating relationships," *Annual Review of Sex Research*, vol. 18, no.1, 2007, pp. 94-114.

2   L. Brown, "How can you tell if your partner has cheated? Here are 16 signs,"

https://ideapod.com/cheating-sleeping-someone-else-9-signs-partner-guilty/

3   K. Kococh and C. Stinchcombe, "17 Signs your partner might be having an affair," July 2022,

https://www.womansday.com/relationships/dating-marriage/advice/a1586/11-signs-that-he-might-be-having-an-affair-107288/

4   "Infidelity," *Wikipedia*, the free encyclopedia

https://en.wikipedia.org/wiki/Infidelity

5   M. Kuroki, "Opposite-sex coworkers and marital infidelity," *Economics Letters*, vol. 118, 2013, pp. 71–73.

6   "Pornography,"

https://www.psychologytoday.com/us/basics/pornography

7   H. A. K. Groothof, P. Dijkstra, and D. P. H. Barelds,

" Sex differences in jealousy: The case of Internet infidelity," *Journal of Social and Personal Relationships*, vol. 26, no. 8, 2009, pp. 1119–1129.

8   "Coping with Infidelity: A life of effectiveness guide,"

http://www.counsellingconnection.com/wp-content/uploads/2011/04/COPING-WITH-INFIDELITY.pdf

9   K. M. Hertlein, J. L. Wetchler, and F. P. Piercy, "Infidelity," *Journal of Couple & Relationship Therapy*, vol. 4, no. 2-3, 2005, pp. 5-16.

10   "10 ways to prevent your marriage from infidelity," August 2020,

https://punchng.com/10-ways-to-prevent-your-marriage-from-infidelity/

11   Boston Counseling Therapy, "Adultery counseling: infidelity

facts, and how to overcome,"

http://thriveboston.com/counseling/adultery-counseling-information-on-adultery-and-how-to-overcome-its-effects/

12   M. Weiner-Davis, "10 things you must know about infidelity and cheating,"

https://www.huffingtonpost.com/michele-weinerdavis/10-things-you-must-know-a_b_7247708.html

13   D. Lusterman, *Infidelity: A Survival Guide.* Oakland, CA: Harbinger Publications, 1998.

14   E. M. Brown, *Patterns of Infidelity and Their Treatment.* Bristol, PA: Taylor & Francis, 1991.

15   D. Carder, *Anatomy of An Affair: How Affairs, Attractions, and Addictions Develop, and How to Guard Your Marriage Against Them.* Moody Publishers, 2017.

CHAPTER 10

UNFORGIVENESS

"Be tolerant of one another and forgive each other if anyone has a complaint against another. Just as the Lord has forgiven you, you also should forgive "
(Colossians 3:13).

Unforgiveness is having a grudge against someone who has offended you. It is not having the willing heart to forgive others. One cannot forgive unless unforgiveness has occurred. Unforgiveness is a reaction to a transgression. It is a "cold" emotion involving resentment, bitterness, anger, fear, and perhaps hatred.[1]

Unforgiving people are their own worst enemy. Negativity cancels out creativity. No good can come out of unforgiveness. It is an enemy of your marriage. It comes in many forms and can manifest as a critical spirit, or bitterness, or wrath, or even irritation. Unforgiveness is the root of many things that separate us from God and others. Some regard it as a curse.[2]

Consider the following quotes on unforgiveness:

"One of the most devastating symptoms of pride is the unwillingness to forgive." — Wayne Gerard Trotman

"Forgiveness is the virtue of the courageous, the response of the forgiven, the mercy of the just." — Ron Brackin

"To violate the law of love is to live in un-forgiveness." — Sunday Adelaja

"Someone once said that unforgiveness was like a poison you drink while hoping for someone else to die." — Jennifer Heng

"When boiled down to its essence, unforgiveness is hatred."
– John R. Rice

CAUSES OF UNFORGIVENESS

As long as we live in this imperfect world, interacting with imperfect people, you are bound to offend someone or someone is bound to offend you. When someone offends you, you have a choice to either forgive or not forgive them. Unforgiveness occurs when you choose not to forgive and be kind to the person who has offended you. It is either doing nothing about the hurt or attempting to punish the transgressor somehow.

The causes of unforgiveness include the following:

1.   The sins and failures of others makes us feel deserving

2.   All the other person's wrongs against us become like a loaded gun that we carry around.

3.   If you are finding it hard to forgive someone, you are likely bottling up anger

4.   It is tempting to usurp God's position and making yourself judge, jury and executioner.

5.   The cost of not allowing the victim off the hook may be a lifetime of unhappiness and bitterness.

6.   Unforgiveness catches us in a snare of Satan.

CONSEQUENCES OF UNFORGIVENESS

The consequences of unforgiveness are deadly and detrimental. These include the following.

1.   *Festers Bitterness:* Unforgiveness does not promote justice. If left untreated, unforgiveness festers into bitterness and resentment, which like poison or cancer can make you physically sick. Randle Lowrance said, "Bitterness is believing God got it wrong, worry is believing God will get it right, and unforgiveness is believing that you are right even after God says you are wrong." Esau held unforgiveness against his brother Jacob. He became embittered against Jacob and was planning to kill him (Genesis 27:41).

2.   *Hurts Relationship:* Unforgiveness blocks love flow in

relationships. Unforgiveness, resentment, and bitterness are spiritual maladies that keep many people from living a Spirit-filled life. They affect our relationships and turn our allies (spouse, children, parents, relatives, friends, co-workers, acquaintances, etc.) into our enemies. They can make us cynical, unable to trust, and unable to maintain close relationships. They give Satan a foothold in our lives. As shown in Figure 1, unforgiveness hurts your relationship.

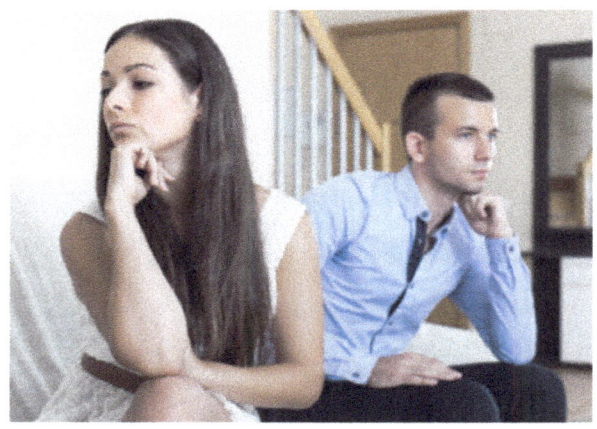

Figure 1 Unforgiveness hurts your relationship.

Source: "Marriage: Drag time—The folly of unforgiveness," June 2014,

https://doingfamilyright.com/drag-time-the-folly-of-unforgiveness/#:~:text=Drag%20time%20is%20the%20difficult,toward%20someone%20close%20to%20you.

3.   *Causes Damage:* Medical practitioners have observed that there is a relationship between forgiveness and health. We suffer alone and in silence when we refuse to allow ourselves to experience God's complete forgiveness. We live in a dangerous cycle of unforgiveness. Unforgiveness can cause spiritual and physical damage. It hurts the one who refuses to forgive. Serious diseases can develop as a result of the poison of unforgiveness put on a person. These may include health challenges such as heart problems, high blood pressure, etc. "They increase the 'bad' (LDL) cholesterol levels and decreasing 'good' (HDL) cholesterol levels. Unforgiveness can decrease the blood flow through the coronary arteries that supply the heart itself."[3] As depicted in Figure 2, unforgiveness can destroy sex in your marriage and affect your marriage bed.

Figure 2 Unforgiveness can destroy sex in your marriage.

Source: J. Sibert, "Is unforgiveness destroying sex in your marriage?" September 2015,

https://intimacyinmarriage.com/2015/09/08/is-unforgiveness-destroying-sex-in-your-marriage/

4.   *Hinders Prayer:* Unforgiveness prevents us from coming into God's presence. It prevents God from forgiving us (Matthew 18:35). God does not want us and our gifts in His presence if we harbor unforgiveness (Matthew 5:24). I do not care how much you know how to pray or what you are going through. Your prayer life is affected by unforgiveness. You only deceive yourself. Your prayer simply won't work in an atmosphere of unforgiveness (Psalm 66:18). God will deal with those who hurt us if we forgive and let Him avenge for us. Vengeance belongs to God (Romans 12:19). Unforgiveness not only hinders prayers, it is one of the major blocks to receiving deliverance and healing from the Lord.

5.   *Gives Room for the Enemy:* The Bible says we should not give place or room for the devil (Ephesians 4:27). Anger and forgiveness give room for the enemy of your marriage. When we fail to forgive, we invite Satan into the situation and give him the opportunity to do harm. He will steal, kill, and destroy your marital happiness if you give him the chance.

FORGIVENESS IS A MUST

Someone has said, "Marriage is the university of all offence, do not marry if you cannot forgive." Marriage needs never ending forgiveness and repentance. The importance of forgiveness in marriage cannot be overstated. Forgiveness is part of the process of restoring hope in a troubled family. The ability to forgive and seek forgiveness is often rated as one of the most important factors that make a relationship last. In a marriage, forgiveness is a must.

Forgiving is the way to deal with unforgiveness. Unforgiveness is a common marital problem, and forgiveness is the solution. Needless to say that forgiveness is a much better way than unforgiveness. Extending forgiveness to those who have hurt us will benefit us more than it will benefit them. Forgiveness is all about giving yourself, your spouse, and your children the kind of future you and they deserve, unhampered by hurt, resentment, and anger. Lewis B. Smedes said, "To forgive is to set a prisoner free and discover that the prisoner was you." Figure 3 shows the keys to forgiveness in a marriage.

Figure 3 The keys to forgiveness in a marriage.

Source: S. Stritof, "How to forgive your partner who has hurt you," July 2023,

https://www.verywellmind.com/forgiveness-and-letting-go-in-marriage-2300611

Forgiveness is simply letting go and building the confidence necessary to experience healthy life. It gives God control, trusts God, and keeps that relationship right. Forgiveness is not only important to save your marriage but to maintain a right relationship with God. It is an active process in which you make a conscious decision to let go of negative feelings whether the person deserves it or not.[4] It is task that requires a transition from negative emotions to positive ones. You will never be able to forgive if you wait until you feel like doing so. Your feelings will need time to catch up with your decision to forgive. Remember that there is no forgiveness for unforgiving people (Matthew 6:14,15).

Some of the characteristics of forgiveness include the following:[5]

- Forgiveness is not letting the offender off the hook.
- Forgiveness is returning to God the right to take care of justice.
- Forgiveness is not letting the offense recur again and again.
- Forgiveness involves not raising the matter again.
- Forgiveness involves change. It is a process, not an event.
- Forgiveness is an indication of true healing.
- Forgiveness takes time. Give yourself time to heal.

DEALING WITH UNFORGIVENESS

Forgiveness is a demonstration of overcoming evil with good and the divine institution for dealing with injustice. It has the power to heal emotional wounds and restore human relationships.[6] The goal of forgiveness is reconciliation with those who offended you, rather than revenge. The following tips will help you to forgive your spouse.

1. *God Demands Forgiveness.* In Matthew 18:21-35, Jesus gave a parable of the unmerciful servant, who was forgiven much by the king but refused to forgive the small debt of another man. Because of this, the king rescinded his prior forgiveness. Jesus concluded by saying, "This is how my heavenly Father will treat each of you unless you forgive your brother or sister from your heart" (Matthew 18:35). Jesus also taught His disciples that unforgiveness is unforgivable (Matthew 6:14). He told Peter that he should forgive indefinitely (Matthew 18:21,22).

Forgiving those who have offended us is never going to be easy because it is a God-like trait to be forgiving. As Alexander Pope said, "To err is human, to forgive, divine." But whenever God asks us to do something, it is always for our benefit. God has given each one of us the ability to forgive those who wrong us. It is up to use to use that ability. Forgiveness is a choice we must make. It is consciously choosing to offer compassion and empathy to the person who wrong us. It takes a major effort of the will to forgive. When we choose to forgive someone, we release the person from his indebtedness to us. We have been given much through forgiveness, and much is expected from us (Luke 12:48). As Ruth Bell Graham said, "A happy marriage is the union of two good forgivers."

2.   *Be quick to forgive:* Someone has said "The first to apologize is the bravest. The first to forgive is the strongest. The first to forget is the happiest." God forgives our sins, puts them as far as the east is from the west, and remembers them no more (Psalm 103:12). In the same way, we His children must learn how to forgive and forget. We are to forgive as soon as possible. Joseph readily forgave his brothers because he knew that God turned their evil plan to good (Genesis 50:20). If God puts it in your mind to forgive someone, be ready to do it. You can do all things through Christ who strengthens you (Philippians 4:13).

3.   *Love Your Enemy:* Do not seek revenge or bear a grudge (Leviticus 19:18). Rather, we are to love our enemies (Matthew 5:44). Although Jesus was tempted in all the ways we are tempted, He forgave. On the cross, He prayer for His enemies: "Father, forgive them. They know not what they do" (Luke 23:34).[7] If you should love your enemy, you should be able to love your spouse, your lover.

4.   *Love Covers a Multitude of Sin:* 1 Peer 4:8 says, "Above all, love each other deeply, because love covers over a multitude of sins." We are to love each other deeply, without holding grudges against one another. This is the agape kind of love; it is sacrificial, not sentimental. It carries the idea of a fervent, unfailing love for each other. The reason for the call to fervent, deep love is because love covers a multitude of sins. The sins of the one loved are covered by the one who loves another. The one who loves overlooks the other person's offenses.[8]

5.   *Pray:* Ask the Lord to give you the power to forgive people who have offended you. "Forgive as the Lord has forgiven you" (Colossians 3:13). Like God did to us, we extend kindness and mercy to others and treat them better than they deserve. Ask God to cleanse and heal you from all of the bitterness, anger and resentment from these hurts and pains. Reconcile with your spouse and pray together

about the issue, as illustrated in Figure 4.

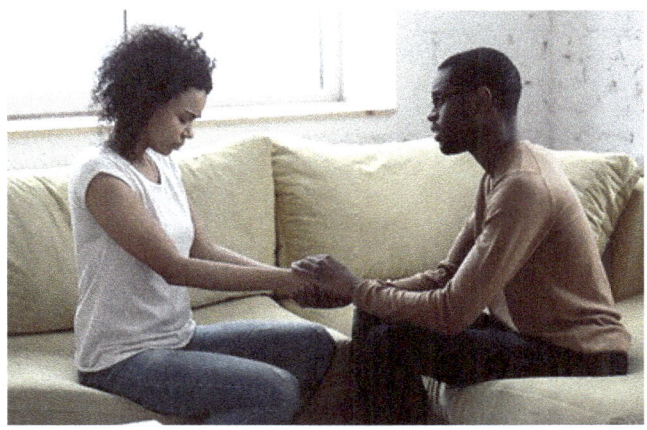

Figure 4 Reconcile and pray with your partner.

Source: T. Gaspard, "The power of forgiveness to save a marriage,"

https://www.divorcemag.com/blog/the-power-of-forgiveness-to-save-a-marriage

6.   *Repent:* Unforgiveness is a sin. Repent of it and allow God to give you the grace empowering you to forgive those that have injured you. When a person genuinely forgives from the heart, they are able to find a sense of peace.

7.   *Forgive in Advance:* We can forgive our spouse in advance because that is why God deals with us. While we were yet His enemies, God sent His Son to die for us (Romans 5:8). He forgave us in advance. If you forgive in advance, you need less reflection and prayer. Deciding ahead of time to forgive those who intentionally or unintentionally hurt us empowers us to move forward without bitterness or pain. It is like stating unconditional love or loving first.[9]

CONCLUSION

As Martin Luther King Jr. said, "Forgiveness is not an occasional act, it is a constant attitude." Forgiveness is the choice we make every day, not based on feelings. It is based on the fact that no spouse is perfect. It may seem unnatural to forgive because fairness demands that people should pay for their wrong doing. But forgiving is love's power to break nature's rule.[10]

Unconditional forgiveness is the ideal; that involves letting go completely of victim. Wise people forgive but do not forget. Do not let unforgiveness control you. Make forgiveness an ally of your marriage. A marriage that practices forgiveness is destined to last and be happy.[11] More information about forgiveness or unforgiveness in marriage can be found in the books.[10-13]

NOTES

1   E. Worthington and N. G. Wade, "The psychology of unforgiveness and forgiveness and implications for clinical practice," *Journal of Social and Clinical Psychology*, vol. 18, no. 4, 1999, pp. 385-418.

2   D. Eells, *The Curse of Unforgiveness.* UBM Books, 2014.

3   "The harmful effects of unforgiveness"

https://whatyourfutureholds.wordpress.com/2009/01/29/the-harmful-effects-of-unforgiveness-benefits-of-forgiving-are-worth-reading-about/

4   "Forgiveness: Your health depends on it,"

https://www.hopkinsmedicine.org/health/healthy_aging/healthy_connections/forgiveness-your-health-depends-on-it

5   R. Swbt, "Forgiveness and restoration," July 2021,

https://www.focusonthefamily.com/marriage/forgiveness-and-restoration/

6   Z. Szablowinski, " Between forgiveness and unforgiveness," *The Heythrop Journal*, 2010, pp. 471–482.

7   E. Worthington et al., "Interpersonal forgiveness as an example of loving one's enemies," *Journal of Psychology and Theology*, vol. 34, no. 1, 2006, pp. 32-42.

8   M. N. O. Sadiku, *1 & 2 Peter: A Pentecostal Commentary.* Bloomington, IN: Trafford Publishing., 2013, p. 78.

9   "Forgive in advance,"

https://www.foodingodsplace.com/forgive-in-advance/#:~:text=If%20you%20forgive%20in%20advance,me%20more%20easily%20without%20distraction.%E2%80%9D

10   L. B. Smedes, *Forgive and Forget.* New York: Harper & Row, 1984, p. xii.

11   T. Ikomi, *Forgiveness Discipleship*: Forgiveness in the Family. New York: Triumph Publishing, 2015.

12   W. Williams, Receiving *Healing Through Forgiveness: A Guide to Freedom.* In His Will Ministries of South Florida, 2021.

13   A. Owens, *The Art of Forgiveness in Marriage: How to Move*

Forward and Build a Stronger Relationship. Independently Published, 2023.

CHAPTER 11

BITTERNESS AND RESENTMENT

"A foolish son is a grief to his father and bitterness to her who bore him"
(Proverbs 17:25, RSV).

Bitterness and resentment often go together and are the result of unresolved anger. While bitterness is a feeling of deep anger and resentment, resentment is often regarded to be synonymous with anger, spite, and other similar emotions. Both of these outcomes are usually expressed outwardly against those around us, especially the ones we love the most.[1]

When you are offended by someone and allow the hurt to germinate in your heart, bitterness and resentment will take root. Feelings of bitterness and resentment are universal. We all experience them at some point in our lives, regardless of our age, race, sex, economic status, etc. Since they are the source of problems in many marriages, they are an enemy of your marriage. In fact, they are the most toxic of all emotions in marriage.

Parents are often the most common victims of bitterness and resentment because they are blamed for most of our failures. Some feel that their parents destroyed their self-esteem, undermined their confidence, and prevented them from achieving anything worthwhile. Criminals are great resenters of their parents.[2]

Resentment in marriage is the buildup of negative feelings towards your partner when you feel wronged, betrayed, neglected, disrespectful, or taken for granted. Bitterness is basically being resentful against someone or something that has caused offense against us. As Gregory Popcak well said, "Bitterness is unforgiveness fermented." It usually starts out in a small way. A person who is bitter is often resentful, cold, and unpleasant to be around. Bitterness is a depressant. Bitter people are unhappy and depressed, hateful, cruel, mean, and hard to deal with. They are miserable and they tend to make others miserable. Listen to the following quotes on bitterness and resentment:

"Bitterness is like cancer. It eats upon the host. But anger is like fire. It burns it all clean." — Maya Angelous

"Bitterness imprisons life; love releases it." – Harry E. Fosdick

"As I walked out the door toward the gate that would lead to my freedom, I knew if I didn't leave my bitterness and hatred behind, I'd still be in prison." — Nelson Mandela

"Resentments are like swallowing poison and expecting the other people to die." — Malachy McCourt

"Harboring resentment is like slapping yourself and then expecting the other person to feel the pain." — Mark Sichel

"Anger, resentment and jealousy doesn't change the heart of others-- it only changes yours." — Shannon L. Alder

"As smoking is to the lungs, so is resentment to the soul; even one puff is bad for you." — Elizabeth Gilbert

CAUSES OF BITTERNESS AND RESENTMENT

These are the common causes of bitterness and resentment in marriage.

1.   *Unfair Treatment:* Bitterness can develop from feeling betrayed, marginalized, or taken advantage of. Resentment is the persistent feeling that one is being treated unfairly. This may be due to painful experiences from home, church or workplace. It may also be caused by a relationship breakup, loss of a job, unfair treatment, discrimination, prejudice, etc. Resentment may be racially motivated. Racial resentment (or symbolic racism) may encompass anger, bitterness, or concern related to one racial group.[3] People who go through life demanding their own way often feel bitter and resentful towards God and others when they feel overlooked or shortchanged.[4]

After losing her husband and two sons, Naomi, the mother-in-law of

Ruth, said, "Things are far more bitter for me than for you, because the LORD himself has caused me to suffer" (Ruth 1:21). Naomi blamed God for her loss and for making her life bitter. She felt God had not been fair to her. She did not realize that God had a plan working behind the scenes. God knew what He was doing. If Naomi's son had not died, Ruth would not have been free marry Boaz and had Obed, the grandfather of David, from whose lineage comes the Messiah Jesus Christ.[5] The Bible says that all things work together for good for those who love God (Romans 8:28).

Like Naomi, the loss of loved ones can create bitterness. I went through that experience when I lost my first wife. She was a wife of my dream and I was embittered for losing her to breast cancer.

2.   *Unresolved Anger:* Bitterness is unresolved, unforgiven anger. Heath Lambert said, " Bitterness is the long term anger that accrues in your life when you refuse to forgive someone who has sinned against you."[6] The moment you start hating a person, you become that person's slave.

3.   *Unforgiveness:* Bitterness can often be traced to unforgiveness. An unwillingness to forgive others is usually at the very heart of bitterness.

4.   *A Root:* Bitterness is a root, and roots are not always visible on the surface (Hebrews 12:15). Bitterness is the root of many problems. From Ephesians 4:31, we can infer that bitterness has many cousins including wrath, anger, clamor, and malice. This is illustrated in Figure 1.

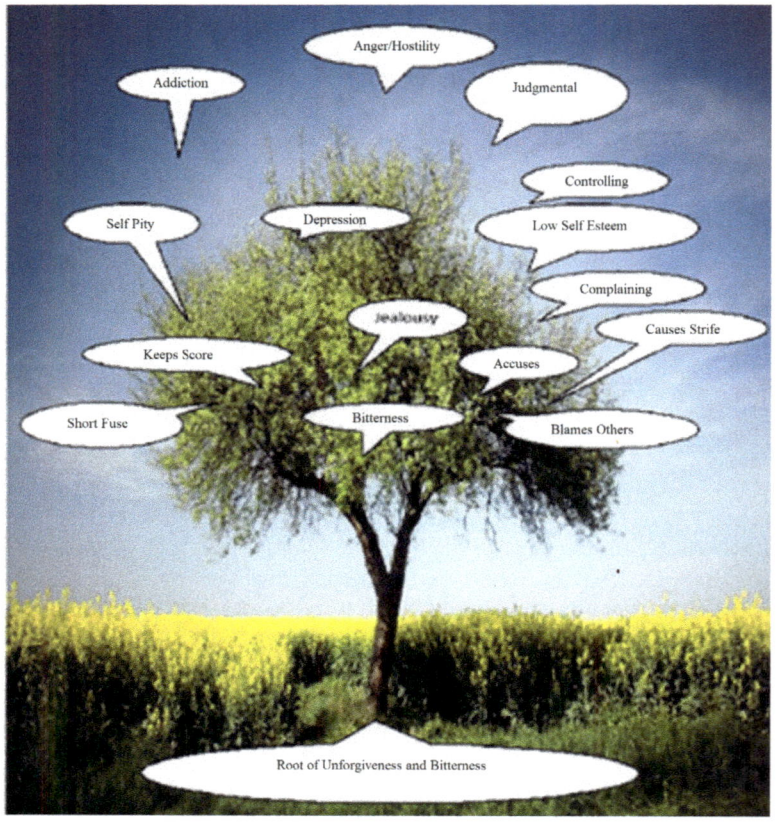

Figure 1 Bitterness is the root of many problems.

Source: "Overcoming bitterness,"

https://healingwordsofjesus.weebly.com/overcoming-bitterness.html

The seed of bitterness is planted when someone does you wrong and the plant grows. Bitterness is a hidden element that lies under the surface, invisible to the eyes. That makes it harder to identify and expose. Demons thrive on bitterness and resentment.[7] As a Latin proverb says, "He who goes angry to bed has the devil for a bedfellow."

The sin of bitterness can do the following:[8]

- It can rob you of your peace and joy.

- It is an open door for Satan to control your life.

- It can lead to the loss of good friends.

- It can hurt or destroy you relationship with your family, your wife and can even lead to the breakup of your home.

- It makes peace and harmony impossible.

- There can be no true biblical love where it exists.

- It destroys any true relationship with the Lord and will keep you from growing in the Lord.

- It will defeat you and ruin your life and the lives of those around you.

This is how you know that you spouse resents you:[9]

1. Withholding sex

2. Lack of affection

3. Increased number and intensity of fights

4. Sadness

5. Feelings of helplessness and hopelessness

6. Reluctance to celebrate milestones

7. Withdrawal from the relationship

EFFECTS OF BITTERNESS AND RESENTMENT IN YOUR MARRIAGE

Bitterness affects you physically, emotionally, socially, and spiritually. It hardens your heart. It is destructive. Bitterness can cause people to begin seeing the world through a negative lens. This negative way of seeing the world and people is isolating. Therefore, we must not allow "bitter roots" to grow in our hearts and cause us to fall short of the grace of God (Hebrews 12:15). The effects of bitterness and resentment include the following:[10,11]

1. *Bitterness Spreads:* Both bitterness and resentment are contagious. Bitterness starts in small way and then spreads and grows. "A little leaven, leavens the whole lump" (Galatians 5:6). It can start to spread throughout your heart and contaminate your whole body. It will start to manifest itself in your attitude, demeanor, and health. The spreading can also affect your spouse and children, the entire family. When you resent people, they resent you too.

2. *Complaining Mode:* Bitterness and resentment put you

in constant "complaining and murmuring mode," complaining excessively. They lead to pity party, creating a bitter, negative outlook of life. When you are bitter, you tend to blame someone else. Most bitter people complain that their offenders have used their power to wrongly hurt them. God does not like us to be complaining and murmuring. He inhabits the praises of His people, not in their complaining. Bitterness invites the devil and his demons into our life.

3. *Creates Unhappiness:* Over time resentment can cause a lot of arguments. Resentment can lead to pain and make it challenging to move on after being wronged by our spouse. Resentment may make family members feel separated and alone. If left unchecked, resentment in marriage is fatal. It can lead to unhappiness and isolation, as illustrated in Figure 2.

Figure 2 Resentment creates an unhappy marriage.

Source: J. Nollan, "7 Simple tips to be happy in an unhappy marriage," June 2023, https://www.aconsciousrethink.com/13452/how-to-be-happy-in-an-unhappy-marriage/

4. *Poisons Marriage:* Bitterness and resentment destroy a marriage. They are stored in the soul and slowly poison the one who carries them. They will poison your emotional life and your marital relationship. A bitter wife or husband does great damage to a relationship. Little by little, day by day, they allow bitterness to poison them. This pattern may go on for years. Eventually, their heart becomes hardened. Do not allow bitterness to take over and poison your marriage.

5. *Hurts Relationship:* Bitterness and resentment affect your

relationships, health, well-being, and career. A wife criticizes her husband unjustly; instead of listening, he nurses resentment. Other resentments accumulate, and the alienation gets broader and wider. We have seen a marriage in which the bitterness had grown so bad that the wife could not sleep at night. Unwillingness to forgive and overlook small offenses will defile your relationship with God and your spouse. This may affect your sexual life, as typically shown in Figure 3.

Figure 3 Resentment may affect your sexual life.

Source: K. Miller and L. Hanrahan, "The 12 biggest reasons for resentment in marriage," March 2020,

https://www.womansday.com/relationships/dating-marriage/advice/g1107/resentment-in-marriage

OVERCOMING BITTERNESS AND RESENTMENT

For sure, you cannot beat bitterness with becoming more bitter or beat resentment by being more resentful. You owe it to yourself to seek to overcome bitterness by taking the following actions.

1.   *Forgive:* First and foremost, you must learn to forgive and let go. The antidote to bitterness and resentment is forgiveness. The solution to bitterness and resent may mean untangling webs that go back for years. It may entail forgiving those who have wronged us. Our lack of forgiveness is why we choose to hold onto bitterness. Forgiveness is a great psychological release, while unforgiveness is a hell-bent sin. It is impossible to go through life without somebody offending us. We must learn to forgive them and move on with our

life.

If we refuse to forgive those who sin against you, God will not forgive us (Matthew 6:15). As Christians, remember that we are forgiven people. As we receive forgiveness, we ought to forgive others too.

Do not listen to those who claim that forgiving is a sign of weakness. Forgiving others is a courageous act that reflects the forgiving, kind, and compassionate attributes of God. As depicted in Figure 4, you need to forgive your partner as you yourself have been forgiven.

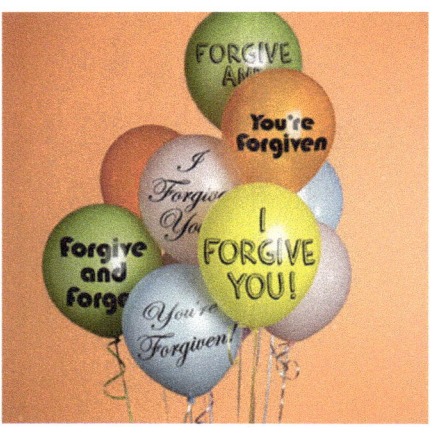

Figure 4   Forgive as you are forgiven.

Source: A. E. Keller, "Forgiveness: How to let go of grudges and bitterness," May 2018,

https://www.dramykellermft.com/blog/2018/5/16/forgiveness-how-to-let-go-of-grudges-and-bitterness

2.   *Be Kind:* To release yourself from bitterness, cultivate loving kindness towards yourself and others. If the bitterness and resentful are due to someone, take the initiative to reconcile. God wants us to be peacemakers (Matthew 5:9). Return love for hurt. Life is too short to hold yourself and others in prison. "Be kind to each other, tenderhearted, forgiving one another, just as God has forgiven you because you belong to Christ" (Ephesians 4:32, TLB). Husbands are asked to love their wives and not be bitter against them (Colossians 3:19). Romans 12:18 says, "If it is possible, as far as it depends on you, live at peace with everyone."

3.   *Communicate:* Being able to communicate your feelings is helpful in overcoming bitterness and resentment. The communication

must be fair to both parties in order to be effective. You resolve your bitterness and resentment through communication. Feel free to communicate your request or even a boundary without blame. Let your talk be coupled with kindness, love and honesty. The Bible says that we should tell the truth in love (Ephesians 4:15). Your goal is to be able to reach some agreement that will help dissolve your bitterness and resentment and move you closer to one each other.

4.	*Seek Help:* If you are still having trouble with bitterness and resentment, I strongly recommend that you seek help of your friends, loved ones, or a counsellor. They may help you process your feelings and shift your perspective. Take responsibility for your actions.

In the same way, the following ways will prevent resentment from destroying your marriage:[12]

1.	Acknowledge your feelings and practice being vulnerable in small steps.
2.	Be honest and communicate about key issues in your relationship.
3.	Take responsibility for your part in the conflict or dispute.
4.	Apologize to your partner when appropriate.
5.	Practice forgiveness.
6.	Show empathy to your partner.
7.	Pray earnestly for your spouse.
8.	Express thoughts, feelings and wishes in a respectful way.
9.	Make a commitment to practice endurance and patience.
10. Replace resentment with compassion and acceptance.

Focus on making your marriage a priority. Spend time together. Boost up your physical affection and sex because physical contact reduces pain and causes a calming sensation. So it is a good idea to have sex because sex is physically connecting and has a way of softening your minds toward each other. Remember that your spouse will not change overnight.

CONCLUSION

A Christian should not be bitter and resentful because bitterness is a rejection of God's sovereignty, plan, and purpose for our lives

(1 Samuel 1:10, Romans 8:28). Resentment is a sin against God and the individual. Because of their destructive nature, bitterness and resentment should be avoided at all costs. They are toxic or poisonous to your marriage. If permitted, they will destroy the relationships with your spouse, children, friends, and even with God. Take prompt and decisive action against bitterness and resentment. More information about bitterness and resentment can be found in the books.[4,13,14]

NOTES

1   R. W. Kahle, "Bitterness and resentment,"

http://www.kindredspiritministries.org/resources/17345.pdf

2   D. Theodore, "The use of resentment," *Psychology Today*, vol. 28, March 1995, pp. 30-32.

3   F. L. Samson, "Racial resentment and smoking," *Social Science & Medicine*, vol. 126, 2015, pp. 164-168.

4   J. I. Wilson, *How to be Free from Bitterness*. Moscow, ID: Canon Press, 2004.

5.   "The heart of bitterness,"

http://biblicalcounselingcoalition.org/2014/02/21/the-heart-of-bitterness/

6   Heath Lambert, "Overcoming bitterness (a transcript)

https://biblicalcounseling.com/2016/12/overcoming-bitterness-transcript/

7   "Root of Bitterness."

http://www.greatbiblestudy.com/bitterness.php

8   "Bitterness,"

http://bible-truth.org/msg162.html

9   L. Howard, "7 signs your partner resents you," https://www.bustle.com/articles/161065-7-signs-your-partner-resents-you

10   S. B. McDonald, "Don't let bitterness poison your marriage,"

https://www.familylife.com/articles/topics/marriage/staying-married/forgiveness/dont-let-bitterness-poison-your-marriage/

11   M. Christensen, "What resentment looks like in a marriage: 8 subtle signs to recognize," July 2023,

https://www.fatherly.com/life/what-resentment-looks-like-in-relationship#:~:text=Clamming%20Up,emotionally%20available%2C%E2%80%9D%20explains%20Decker.

12   T. Gaspard, "Is resentment ruining your marriage?"

https://www.huffingtonpost.com/terry-gaspard-msw-licsw/is-resentment-ruining-your-marriage_b_5531600.html

13   S. Anderson, *A Guide On How To Overcome Bitterness And Resentment In Life And In Marriage: 8 Practical Steps To Overcome That Deep-Seated Feeling Of Sadness, Anger, Pessimism, And Hopelessness*. Kindle Edition, 2022.

14   R. D. Jones, *Freedom from Resentment: Stopping Hurts from Turning Bitter*. New Growth Press, 2010.

CHAPTER 12

OVERCOMMITMENT

"Nobody on his deathbed ever said, 'I wish I had spent more time on my job.'"
— Paul Tsongas

Overcommitment is plaguing our society and our marriage is unfortunately the first casualty. Experts have cited overcommitment as one of the top five relationship killers. Dr. James Dobson, a noted psychologist in California, has noted: "The most dangerous threat to family life is one seldom mentioned. We can talk about alcoholism, drug abuse or infidelity, but a more common threat is the simple matter of overcommitment." He continues, "I'm talking about the husband and wife who are too exhausted to take walks together, understand one another, meet each other's needs, have time for play, have time for children, have time for devotions. The husband often moonlights to maintain some standard of living; the wife works and tries to oversee the home; everyone is on the brink of exhaustion."[1]

Overcommitment is obliging to do more than one is capable. It may be regarded as a set of attitudes, behaviors and motions that reflect a person's excessive striving for approval and appreciation. It is the inability to withdraw from obligations at work.[2] Overcommitted individuals are doing way too much, trying to handle a hundred things at once. They are very ambitious and tend to exaggerate their efforts while at the same time over- tax their resources.

You may be a superman or a high-achieving woman. You may not be a good material for marriage. Overcommitment, busyness, time pressure, is an enemy of your marriage. An overcommitted To Do List is shown in Figure 1.

Figure 1 Overcommitted To Do List.

Source: P. Bongiorno, Are You Overcommitted?" July 2016,

https://www.psychologytoday.com/us/blog/inner-source/201607/are-you-overcommitted#:~:text=Defining%20and%20Studying%20Overcommitment&text=People%20who%20are%20overcommitted%20generally,of%20exhaustion%20and%20poor%20health.

Here are some signs indicating that you are overcommitting yourself:[3]

- You are starting to make spelling or math errors
- You are neglecting to eat
- You get easily irritated
- You are putting in more time but getting less done
- Nothing outside of work receives your attention
- You are not sleeping enough
- You are having trouble managing your time and completing projects

CAUSES OF OVERCOMMITMENT

Just about any adult you talk to struggles with busyness and stress. It may be due to involvement in church activities, being involved in children extracurricular activities, serving as organization's board members, taking some college classes, husband and wife are busy at work, invitation to attend an event, shopping, maintaining a supper clean house, taking charge of health through exercising, visiting relatives, etc. Overcommitment, overpromising, overextending, and overdoing do not help us live a balanced life. Some of the causes of overcommitment include busyness, lack of goals and priorities, pleasing others, selfishness, lack of divine direction, and ambition, trying to achieve too much.

1.   *Busyness:* Sometimes life can be very busy due to circumstances outside of our control. You are too busy. Your to-do list has exploded. You find yourself overbooked for several activities. You are overcommitted and overwhelmed. You may even find yourself putting in extra hours at night when you would normally be sleeping.

2.   *Lack of goals and priorities:* It is easy to get distracted and follow the crowd when we do not have personal goals and priorities to achieve the goals. Someone has said that goals are the oxygen to our dreams. They are the first steps to every journey we take. If you don't plan your life, others will decide for you.

3.   *Pleasing others:* We seek to gain other people's approval. We find it hard to say no to their requests. Overcommitted people excessively strive for approval and appreciation. But people-pleasing attitude can run havoc in their marriage. Without knowing it, they let their marriage suffer at the expense of doing a favor for others.

TYPES OF OVERCOMMITMENT

Overcommitment has been tied to several mental and physical health issues. It can manifest itself in different aspects of our life, resulting in different types of overcommitment. It is a widespread issue affecting people's domestic, work, social, spiritual, financial, political, and digital life, causing stress, anxiety, and constant sense of overwhelming. We discuss these in detail as follows:[3-8]

1.   *Domestic Overcommitment:* We often find yourselves overcommitting to all the various things surrounding our domestic life. Overcommitment often leaves us ignoring our basic needs. Overcommitting as a homemaker is an easy trap to fall in. Imagine a working parent trying to balance a demanding career with domestic duties. Overcommitted moms are called different names: Super mom, Tiger mom, Helicopter mom. Overachiever mom, etc. Figure 2 shows an overcommitted working parent.

Figure 2 An overcommitted working parent.

2.   *Work Overcommitment:* Becoming overwhelmed with work is a reality for many. Workaholism and overcommitment are terms that are often used interchangeably to describe an individual's over-involvement toward their job. They describe workers who tend to work excessively and sacrifice their personal life in favor of extra-involvement in work. People often overestimate their productivity or their ability to multitask. Overcommitment often leaves us ignoring our basic needs. For example, consider a young professional who spends their weekends hunched over a laptop, catching up on work instead of indulging in a hobby or simply relaxing. This type of overcommitment wreaks havoc on our mental state and marriage, causing stress, worry, and feelings of being overwhelmed. When your plate is too full, the quality of your work can suffer. Recognizing overcommitment and taking steps to control it can help regain balance in our lives. Figure 3 shows a lady who is overcommitted at work.

Figure 3 Overcommitment at work.

Source: "The culture of overcommitment,"

https://ymemerson.com/new-blog-2/2017/7/28/the-culture-of-overcommitment

3.   *Social Overcommitment:* Some people cultivate the habit of going out every weekend for parties. We often feel obligated to agree to every request that comes our way. Someone might feel compelled to attend social events more out of obligation than interest. A working parent might find their weekends filled with invitations to social events, leaving little or no time for family. A person may find themselves at multiple parties and occasions, not because they enjoy them, but because they fear disappointing their friends if they fail to show up. You must weigh the value and importance of an occasion before agreeing to an invitation.

4.   *Spiritual Overcommitment:* There is nothing wrong with being energetic, purposeful, zealous, or excited about the things of God. The danger comes when we do more than we can handle. In the name of serving the Lord, we become overcommitted spiritually. There are times when we can find ourselves involved in too many religious activities and juggling too many responsibilities in the church. Overcommitment can damage our spiritual success. It is God's will that we do the tasks He has given us to do, not more and not less. Exodus 18 provides us with a very important truth about the dangers of overcommitting ourselves. Moses' father-in-law, Jethro, paid him a visit. Jethro noticed that Moses spent from morning until evening judging the people of Israel. Jethro then advised Moses to divide the labor between many other faithful, trustworthy men so that he

would only have to decide the most difficult of cases. Moses listened, delegated, and avoided the dangers of overcommitment.

5.   *Financial Overcommitment:* Financial overcommitment occurs when your income can no longer meet the bills coming in or when there is a drop in income. It is easy to become financially overcommitted. By careful budgeting, planning, having goals, being realistic about what you can afford, and determination to get out debt, you can avoid debt problems and make the most of your income. By shopping around and negotiating, you can make your money go further.

6.   *Political Overcommitment:* America has a political overcommitment problem. There is little or no consensus on how to deal with this problem. Washington has repeatedly made the mistake of making promises around the world it cannot keep. There is a growing consensus that the United States is overextended. We are formally committed by treaty to defending more countries than at any time in US history. Our global leadership is taking its toll on the economy.

7.   *Digital Overcommitment:* Modern societies are increasingly dependent on technology. Technology is everywhere. It surrounds every aspect of 21st-century life. It is in the cell phones we use, the cars we drive, and even the food we eat. Digital technologies play an ever-increasing role in our daily lives. They have transformed home, work, shopping, music, movies, television, photography, travel, transportation, manufacturing, and communications. Digital overcommitment or addiction refers to an impulse control disorder that involves the obsessive use of digital devices, digital technologies, and digital platforms, i.e. Internet, video game, online platforms, mobile devices, digital gadgets, and social network platform. It is a harmful dependence on digital media and devices. The vast majority of digital natives are addicted to technology, as it is typically shown in Figure 2.

Figure 4 Addiction to technology.

Source: "Life in the age of internet addiction,"

https://theweek.com/articles/468363/life-age-internet-addiction

EFFECTS OF OVERCOMMITMENT

Overcommitment is not good for you marriage. It can lead to loss of credibility/integrity, stress, health-related problems, and bad marriage.

1.   *Loss of Credibility:* We like to be men and women of integrity. Whenever you fail to live to up to your commitments, it hurts your credibility and the level of trust others have in you. When you say yes instead of no, it is difficult to be trusted to fulfill your commitments. Your track record for fulfilling your commitments is critical to building your credibility.[9]

2.   *Stress:* Stress and burnout are expected outcomes of overcommitment to work over time. Work-related stress is associated with an increased risk for cardiovascular disease. Overcommitted persons often judge their work situations as more demanding than less committed persons. They are driven by their high need for approval and appreciation, thereby precipitating stress and exhaustion in the long run. The demands they place upon themselves may lead to increased levels of stress.[10] To avoid stress, being overwhelmed and overcommitted should not be a normal part of your professional life.

3.   *Health problems:* Overcommitment can lead to depression, diabetes, sleep problems, poor blood sugar control, inflammatory

disease, and cardiovascular disease. It can lead to the mental state of vital exhaustion, which is characterized by unusual fatigue, irritability, and demoralization and an established predictor of heart disease. It may also cause sleep problems such as sleep disturbances, insomnia, and poor sleep quality.

4.   *Bad marriage:* Overcommitment is not good for your marriage. It makes you sacrifice things that are irreplaceable. These include values and relationships – between spouses, parents/children, friends, etc. Overcommitment does not provide time for husband and wife to communicate with each other, pray together, enjoy a sexual relationship, or raise kids together. Overcommitted individuals do not live a balanced life and cannot give to their spouse and children what they need.

AVOIDING OVERCOMMITMENT

While it is good to have a passion and a dream, it should be kept in balance with other valuable components of your life. Learning to break the pattern of overcommitment requires discipline and patience. Realizing that time is a finite commodity, you must keep your life in balance. The following tips will help you achieve this and avoid overcommitment.

1.   *Prioritize:* We must apply wisdom on how we spend our precious time. We must prioritize our commitments. Here are three levels of commitment in order of importance:[11]

(1) Commitment to God

(2) Commitment to family

(3) Commitment to others, work, ministry or vocation

This indicates that you need to spend more time with God and your partner and kids. A lot of people mix up the order and run into trouble. Being able to set priorities and allocate time appropriately are critical time management skills we must develop.

Select what is more important and focus on them. Be realistic and avoid last-minute commitments. Delegate what you can. Learn from past experience to balance your commitments in the future. It is very difficult if not impossible to have it all — the career, the family, the social life, the spiritual life, etc. You need to figure out what you value most, and allocate your time and money to pursing them.

2.   *Learn to say No:* Once you know what your priorities are, learn to say no to other commitments. Learning to say may be difficult, but we must learn it. Before you say yes to an opportunity to serve, count the cost and ask yourself if the commitment is going to cut into my time with God and my family. For every commitment you make, you put your integrity on the line. Turn down new opportunities to serve if they would stretch you too thin.

3.   *Rest more:* Sleep rejuvenates our body and reduces stress. Sleep is important for various activities of brain function such as cognition, concentration, productivity, and performance. Each of these activities is negatively impacted by sleep deprivation.[12] Failure to reserve some time for enough rest (as Jesus did) is risking even the good things we are committing ourselves to. Busyness is one of Satan's tools that he uses to distract us from contentment.

CONCLUSION

The America's breathless lifestyle is unacceptable. It is not healthy for your marriage. Make every effort to resist the temptation of overcommitment. For the sake of your marriage and family, you should not overcommit yourself. Do not let overcommitment crowd out your valued relationships. Instead, husband and wife should be fully committed to what God has purposed for their marriage.

NOTES

1   B. Barlow, "Overcommitment labeled no. 1 threat to marriages," https://www.deseretnews.com/article/40211/OVERCOMMITMENT-LABELED-NO-1-THREAT-TO-MARRIAGES.html

2   D. Preckel et al., "Overcommitment to work is associated with vital exhaustion," International Archives of Occupational and Environmental Health, vol. 78, no. 2, March 2005, pp. 117–122.

3   D. Zahariades, "7 Signs you're overcommitted," https://artofproductivity.com/7-signs-youre-overcommitted/

4   L. Ho, "Signs you're overcommitted & how to stop it," https://www.lifehack.org/932490/overcommitting

5   "Avoiding overcommitment," https://ear.powerflexweb.com/tipsheetsUK/tipsheetsDetailEmailTSN.php?recid=47258&searchType=body&searchCriteria=budget&language=English&department=tsn

6   "Exodus 18 – Jethro's counsel to Moses," https://enduringword.com/bible-commentary/exodus-18/

7   M. N. O. Sadiku, S. M. Musa, and O. D. Olaleye, Digital Everything: A Primer – Volume 1. Moldova, Europe: Lambert Academic Publishing, 2023, p. 4.

8   S. M. Walt, "America has a commitment problem," https://foreignpolicy.com/2019/01/29/america-has-a-commitment-problem/

9   "Two keys to avoid over-commitment," http://www.andersonleadershipsolutions.com/two-keys-to-avoiding-over-commitment/

10   Å. B. Rennesund and P. Ø. Saksvik, "Work performance norms and organizational efficacy as cross-level effects on the relationship between individual perceptions of self-efficacy, overcommitment, and work-related stress," European Journal of Work and Organizational Psychology, vol.19, no. 6, 2010, pp. 629-653.

11   M. N. O. Sadiku and J. O. Sadiku, Secrets of Successful Marriages. Bloomington, IN: iUniverse, 2nd edition, 2022, p. 168.

12   J. Leech, "10 reasons why good sleep is important,"

https://www.healthline.com/nutrition/10-reasons-why-good-sleep-is-important#section1

CONCLUSION

You can have a solid, dynamic, happy marriage if you are willing to pay the price. A lasting relationship involves sacrifice, serving, giving, and forgiving. Marriage takes work, commitment, and courage. It takes addressing the twelve problems discussed in this book. Be willing to talk about the problems and their solutions with your spouse. Remember that the goal of a successful marriage is for husband and wife to become their best friends.

Although twelve problems have been identified in this book as enemies of happy marriages, there are other problems which time and space would not permit us include. These include excessive debt/credit, abuse and misuse of money, interference from in-laws, incompatibility, putting sex on the back burner, domestic violence, drug and alcohol abuse, boredom, unrealistic expectations, and the list continues. We believe that these problems are not as devastating on your marriage as the twelve mentioned in the book. The problems addressed in this book are the top 12 problems. If you overcome them, others will take care of themselves. If you address them or avoid them, you will enjoy your marriage and be happy. As Albert Einstein said, "A clever person solves a problem. A wise person avoids it."

INDEX

www.ingramcontent.com/pod-product-compliance
Lightning Source LLC
Chambersburg PA
CBHW041628140626
46547CB00031B/1250